Don't be the Ugly Duckling at the Peacock Party:

Why Waddle when You Can Strut?

Sharon A. Hill

Online editions may be available for this title. For more information visit www.lulu.com.

ISBN: 978-0-578-04076-9

Acknowledgements

As always…

To my beloved husband, Elmer Hill

Contributors

Dave Baldwin

Heidi Brooks

Bud Bilanich

Berta Campbell

Kim Campbell

Kim Caroselli

Phyllis Davis

R. Eaton II

Elmer Hill

Lee Holliday

Terri Houston

Wendi Lester

Burton King

Jeannie Mellinger

Jeff Mudgett

Phil Okrend

Lorana Price

Jeff Snell

Lori Wagoner

Kim Walker

Nicole Warren

Wikipedia and WikiAnswers

Table of Contents

Prologue

Successful people create positive personal impact. People with positive personal impact are easy to spot. They are the ones that everyone wants to work with. They exude a certain magnetism that draws others to them.

Developing and nurturing your unique personal brand is the first thing you need to do to create positive personal impact. Reduce personal branding to two very simple steps. First, figure out how you want others to think of you. Second, make sure that everything you do creates and reinforces this mental image in the minds of others.

Dressing for success is the second thing you need to do to create positive personal impact. Look good. Take pride in your appearance. Dress a little better than you have to. Look in the mirror as you are leaving for the day. Ask yourself, "Does the way I look show respect for myself and the people I'll meet today?" If the answer is "yes," go on and have a great day. If the answer is "no," take a few minutes to change before you head out the door.

Your on-line presence is important too. A Career Builder survey showed that 45% of employers use Google and social networking sites when they are evaluating job candidates. Make sure that your on-line image is as buttoned up and together as your personal appearance.

Finally, all that stuff your mom told you about being polite is true. You can never go wrong by acting like a lady or gentleman. Ladies and gentlemen display good manners and they know and follow the rules of etiquette.

Manners are simply about being a nice and kind person. Etiquette is about rules. Learn the basic rules of etiquette. If you know the rules, you do not have to worry about what to do in a social or business situation. You can concentrate on the business at hand and be comfortable.

The most important rule, however, is to do whatever you can to make the people around you feel comfortable. Do not embarrass others who do not know the rules. Being right is no excuse for embarrassing someone else. You build friendships when you create positive personal impact – and friends can help you get where you want to go.

Bud Bilanich

The Common Sense Guy

Follow on Twitter: http://twitter.com/BudBilanich

303 393 0446 -- Office

303 868 2531 -- Mobile

Bud@BudBilanich.com

www.BudBilanich.com

www.CommonSenseCoach.com

www.CommonSenseKeynotes.com

www.SuccessCommmonSense.com (blog)

Introduction

Ah, the poor ugly duckling. When out of its element, it is awkward, insecure, and often ridiculed because it does not fit in. The same applies to everyday people who have missed etiquette training and find themselves in situations in which they feel out of their comfort zone. Worse yet are people who have no idea that they are being perceived as ugly ducklings due to a lack of etiquette education.

Their eating habits make the meal uncomfortable for fellow diners. They show undesirable telephone and email behaviors. They do not know how to socialize in polite society. The list is exhaustive for the ugly duckling.

Now, consider the peacocks. They are confident, considered attractive and desirable. They surround themselves with other peacocks and are always in their element no matter where they are or what they are doing. Peacocks are the people who have learned, and practice, proper etiquette in all situations. They know how to present themselves and how to treat others with respect and courtesy.

Peacocks are gracious to all, but they may not invite the ugly duckling back to their party. Therefore, don't you be the ugly duckling at the peacock party.

My first etiquette book, *Wild Woman's Guide to Etiquette: Saving the World One Handshake at a Time*, presented basic etiquette tips to help people become comfortable in social and business environments. Since its publication, I have received hundreds of follow-up etiquette questions. Those questions, combined with the questions asked at my etiquette workshops, presentations and questions sent to my etiquette mailbox manners@sharonhillinternational.com, inspired *Don't be the Ugly Duckling at the Peacock Party: Why Waddle when You Can Strut?*

As you read this book and find that you are the ugly duckling in some of the situations listed, practice the etiquette tips to transform yourself. Change your waddles to struts. Practice makes perfect.

Preface

History of Etiquette

The idea of etiquette rules goes back to the times when people began to live in groups and understood that it was better to get along with one another than to quarrel or fight. The first rules for proper social behavior were developed in ancient Greece and Rome. The French royal courts in the late seventeenth century created much of today's formal etiquette.

For example, shaking hands is one of earliest forms of etiquette. By giving somebody his hand, a warrior wanted to show that he did not have any weapons and came in peace.

The nobles who lived at court did not work, so they developed elaborate social customs to avoid becoming bored. The nobles drew up a list of proper social behaviors and called it etiquette. This word came from an old French word meaning ticket. This code of behavior soon spread to other European courts and eventually was adopted by the upper classes throughout the Western world.

Each culture has its own system of etiquette that can sometimes vary greatly among different societies. Behavior that is proper in one culture may be improper in another. For example, it is proper etiquette to remove one's shoes when entering a home in Japan, but it is not something expected in all countries. In addition, what is considered proper in a city could be considered improper in a small town.

The first recordings of American etiquette were made in George Washington's Rules of Civility, but Emily Post wrote the most popular "first" about manners in 1922. The self-proclaimed debutante-turned-writer published Etiquette--In Society, In Business, In Politics, and At Home. It became a best-seller and paved the way for her successors to continue preaching good manners.

Section 1. Everyday Etiquette

Difference between an Ugly Duckling and a Peacock

Ugly ducklings consider themselves the center of the universe. They do not give a second thought to:

- Butting in line

- Letting an elderly person stand instead of offering a seat on a bus or train

- Screaming into a cell phone on an airplane

- Letting the elevator door close as a person is clearly running to catch that elevator

- Treating wait staff like 2nd class citizens

- Using coarse language around people who are outside their inner circle of ugly ducklings

- Eating like Neanderthals

- Not saying please or thank you

- Behaving badly in both business and social environments.

Every time they waddle, they diminish their professionalism and respect.

To the peacock, the universe centers on others. They realize that if others feel comfortable being with them they have elevated their respect and professionalism. Peacocks practice every-day etiquette and basic manners because, in civilized society, they know they are always being watched. Consciously or unconsciously, they want to display a cultured upbringing and a respect for others. When peacocks strut, people watch, listen and admire.

Making a Positive First Impression

Ugly ducklings are not limited to one class of people. You will find them in the ranks all the way up to CEOs, MBAs, Ph.D.s, sports heroes, A-list actors and politicians. Remember, the majority consider themselves the center of the universe. Many covet money and power, giving little or no thought to courtesy and etiquette.

However, some ugly ducklings are people with good hearts who were never taught etiquette, thus unaware of the bad first impression they have made.

Peacocks know it takes between 3 to 10 seconds to make an impression (positive or negative). Peacocks know the tips, especially in business, to make a positive impression.

Business Introductions

Want to know a sure-fire way to insult someone innocently? Try an improper introduction. Remember, as a poised and professional ugly duckling or peacock, you are always being watched. The last thing you want to do is leave a negative impression with a client, potential client or business professional. They will not mention it; but your name may become lodged in their memory as a person who could use etiquette training.

Introducing people does not merely mean informing each party the name of the other. It is the duty of the person making the introduction to ensure they have created a friendly, cordial and warm atmosphere. Do you want to show your respect, but are not sure of the basic protocol of introduction? It is easy when you follow this simple advice: use the name of the higher-ranking person first. Equate ranking to the military. General Stephens, I would like you to meet Sgt. Charles Wilson. Colonel Sandra Rosser, I would like you to meet Master Sgt. Anthony Powell.

Translate the process to business. If Cari Willis is a CEO that you want to introduce to one of your employees, Adine Simmons, the introduction would be: Cari, I'd like you to meet Adine Simmons.

Knowing a person is a CEO makes introductions easy, but it is important to be aware of the many subtleties of introductions. In business situations, know the first and last names of both people you are introducing and take care to pronounce each person's name correctly. If you are like most people, you will experience a brain cramp on the name of someone you see every day. If the group is wearing nametags, sneak a peek to remind you. This is an art form, which when done gracefully, can be your little secret. If there is no nametag, and no one is handy to remind you of the forgotten name, be honest. Say something like, "I can't believe it. I just drew a blank on your name!" As a peacock, take responsibility for forgetting a name.

The ugly duckling leaves people in an uncomfortable situation by introducing them, then just walking away, leaving them in the position of not knowing what to say. The peacock knows some piece of pertinent information about each person that will bring relevance to the introduction. The information provided could pertain to the reason the person is a special guest, or it could highlight a particular accomplishment, hobby, etc. As with any introductions, be a peacock and be discreet. Do not say anything that would embarrass the guest or those being introduced.

Business Card Etiquette

Because people are protective of their email addresses and other contact information, the ugly duckling errs by asking someone for their card without giving a specific reason for requesting it. Still, after telling someone why you want his or her card, he or she may or may not give it to you.

It is awkward to ask for a business card and then watch a person pat down a shirt, back pocket, or purse and say, "I don't have one with me." The truth is, he or she may have one; but does not want you to have it. It is far better to tell someone your reason for wanting a card before asking for it. He or she may still refuse you the card; but it is less awkward and you will know why.

For example, if you explain you would like to call them about your product, they may tell you, "I'm not the person to contact about this. I suggest you call Ralph Wilder in our purchasing department."

Just as there is a hierarchy for initiating a handshake with a senior executive, the same hierarchy exists for the business card. Do not ask a senior executive for a business card. Senior executives who want you to have their card will generally have a specific reason for giving it to you.

Your card is personal. Avoid passing it out randomly or forcing it on anyone who does not want it.

Networking Etiquette Dos and Don'ts

How to Break Out of a Conversation

The ugly duckling bolts. The peacock goes into interview mode asking the other person's favorite band, best part of their job, weirdest childhood fear— anything to bring out inner coolness. The conversation may turn into an enjoyable discussion.

If you just want out, a short-and-sweet "nice talking to you" works best. You do not need to make up a lie. You could get busted on it, or worse, have the person tag along with you.

If you feel like you need a reason to leave, just say you want to say hello to a friend or get another drink. To make the excuse more believable, do what you said you were going to do. And if you run into that person again, just smile and keep moving.

How to Break Into a Conversation

The peacock stands at the perimeter of a group and listens to the conversation, and when it is appropriate, asks if he or she may join them. You will be welcomed into the conversation. Give your opinion on whatever they are talking about, or ask a question. Be cordial and non-confrontational. Smile.

It is often best to start with a small comment and judge the reaction before continuing.

Understand, if you do not know what they are talking about; but it sounds interesting, you should ask the group about it and then stay in the questioning mode.

If you walk in on a conversation and have no clue what they are talking about, do not say anything until you have figured it out or you risk saying something stupid and can become an ugly duckling.

If you know the people who are talking, they will be more likely to let you join. However, if anyone hints to go away, you should.

Try to see what kind of conversation it is before jumping in. Avoid those having a personal conversation. Do not linger near one too long, as they might consider you nosy. Avoid political discussions unless you are positive you agree with their views.

Try to read the body language of the people talking. Before you join, see if the people are speaking closely or in hushed tones. If it seems to be a serious conversation, you might want to leave them alone. If the group seems more open, take the opening. If the members of the conversation try to nudge you out, take the hint and assume the conversation was personal in nature.

The biggest conversation-killer is appearing nervous and unconfident. Do not worry about saying something stupid; it happens to all of us at some point. The worst thing you can do is NOT to speak up when there is a fitting opportunity.

Do not repetitively barge in on multiple conversations at one event. People might consider you to be nosy, and that will be used against you often when you try to join future conversations. Plus, if you do barge in on personal conversations, you will probably receive negative feedback from the conversers.

Business vs. Social Etiquette

Should the man always pull the chair out for the woman at the formal dinner? Should men stand during a meal when a woman leaves or returns to the table? Should the woman always be introduced first when meeting new people?

Ugly ducklings do not have a clue about the importance of these questions. Peacocks, however, know that the answers depend upon whether the situation is business or social.

Before women became a strong force in the business world, the answer to all the questions was yes. However, now that women are in the boardroom, have their own businesses, are project managers, and are (in most cases) on par with men in the business world, the answer is no for business situations. Treat the woman as you treat the man. Gone are the days of women being considered as delicate lasses with parasols and fainting couches. Women are fighter pilots, boxers, fire fighters, CEOs, top salespeople, and entrepreneurs.

Therefore, in business situations peacocks do not apply all the rules of social situations.

Caveat: Some business women appreciate having the gentleman open doors for her and standing when she approaches the formal dining table. Get to know people and adjust accordingly to be a peacock that makes a positive impression in social and business situations.

Handshake Etiquette

In my book *Wild Woman's Guide to Etiquette: Saving the World One Handshake at a Time*, I explain the essentials of an effective handshake, especially to make a positive first impression. Ugly ducklings have a wet or sweaty right hand, give weak or limp handshakes, squeeze too hard, or only offer their fingertips instead of their entire right hand.

Over the many centuries of human existence, many social customs have emerged out of both necessity and leisure. The handshake is one custom that encompasses both of those origins. The handshake may appear little more than a formality to some, but to others it is a complete view into the personality of the person on the other end of the handshake. The handshake has also created nations and bought homesteads. However, in all cases it still requires two people to be executed correctly, thus causing an interaction to take place.

Hugs vs. Handshakes

The #1 follow-up question from my Pump Up Your Professionalism seminars concerns hugs vs. handshakes. Peacocks extend their hand for a warm, personable handshake only to find themselves in an unexpected bear hug. When I ask for a show of hands for hugger and non-huggers, about 45% of my audiences raise hands indicating they are huggers. I point out that not everyone is a hugger and we must be considerate of that fact. The question becomes: how do you avoid a hug and not offend?

The answer involves delicate physical prowess. Usually, the first time you find yourself in a hug, it is a surprise. My answer explains how to handle subsequent unwanted hug attempts. As the hugger is approaching you, extend your right arm and hand for the handshake. Convert your right arm into a steel rod that will not bend at the elbow. Plant your right foot in front of you, directly under your right arm. Do not shift or move as the potential hugger approaches you. Smile. Ideally, this is a signal to the hugger that you prefer a handshake and not a hug.

However, some huggers are stealthy and manage to encroach into your steely stance. Immediately cross your right shoulder across your body into the hugger's right shoulder. Pat the hugger gently on the back and break the hug. You are now the peacock who has engineered a quasi-hug, ensuring your body is respected without offending the hugger.

One more approach to avoid a hug is to place your left hand on their right shoulder and gently push their right shoulder away from you as you smile and shake hands. You want to maintain your poised and professional demeanor to make a positive impression.

If all else fails, tell the hugger (during the embrace), "I am usually not a hugger." Say it in a friendly manner with the hope the hugger gets the message.

Handling People Who Don't Shake Hands

You extend your hand for a handshake and find the person does not extend his hand to shake your hand. Now what? Is that person an ugly duckling with no social grace? Nope. The person could be a germaphobe or just a person who does not like to shake hands.

Your response to this potentially uncomfortable situation is to be a peacock, by lowering your right hand to your side and continue the conversation as if nothing has happened.

Show respect by not asking about what just happened with the non-handshake. For future encounters, you now know not to offer this person a handshake.

Entering a Person's Space

Handshake etiquette does have certain subtleties that separate the ugly duckling from the peacock. We all know that whoever offers the handshake first has the "power." However, there are exceptions.

For example, when you walk into someone's office, cubicle, or space, protocol says you are to wait until that person offers a handshake first. This non-maneuver shows deference to that person's space. Plus, what if the person just sneezed or doesn't like to shake hands? Not offering your hand saves an uncomfortable situation.

If, however, a person enters your space and you are a hand shaker, offer your handshake immediately.

Sneezing and Dirty Hands

You are a peacock being approached by a friend who is offering a handshake. There is one problem. You just sneezed and do not have a tissue handy. As a peacock you know that the proper maneuver is for you to say, "Apologies, but I just sneezed and don't want to give you my germs."

Of course, your friend appreciates your honesty and tact. An ugly duckling would have just shaken hands and not given the situation a second thought.

This brings up another point. Peacocks always have a tissue or handkerchief handy.

Dining Irritations

My book, *Wild Woman's Guide to Etiquette: Saving the World One Handshake at a Time,* discusses dining etiquette in detail. For this book, I want to help civilization display poise and polish throughout its dining experience. I asked others for input into gross, disturbing, or just plain ugly duckling behavior in restaurants.

The respondents range from patrons, servers, and restaurant management personnel. Here is what they offered:

From R. Eaton II:

I have not worked as a server, but I've managed a restaurant. One of the things I had a big problem with, and still have problems with, is "blowing of the nose" at the table with their napkin while continuing to eat afterwards. This is the most sickening thing that one can do.

You have a person eating something like soup, and then across the aisle from you is someone blowing his nose. You can hear him as he blows all the "mucus" out of his nostrils due to the loudness of the blowing.

Now, as a medical professional, I know that this is unsanitary. However, some people who do this type of action seem not to care at all and think it is good etiquette. I beg to differ! This is just nasty and gross!!

From Jeff Snell:

As part owner of Savoy in North Raleigh, North Carolina, a 4-star rated white-table cloth restaurant, I would like to see a section on tipping.

Our wines are priced below most restaurants, but many people seem to think it's okay not to tip on alcohol "because it's already overpriced." Well, it is not always at every restaurant and we happen to have a restaurant host/sommelier and two executive chefs that invest a lot of time and effort in learning about our wine selections, pairing correctly with foods, and educating our guests.

Don't want to leave 20% on an $8 beer at the hockey game? Fine, but do not stiff a professional wait staff on a $24 bottle of wine that should cost $24 at a restaurant!

Similarly, nicer restaurants will not charge a cork fee for a high-end bottle or bottle not offered by the establishment. However, it is beyond tacky to bring cheap wine for the express purpose of saving a buck. Expect to pay (and tip on) a cork fee if you are bringing a bottle less than $50 retail at a wine store. Don't even think about bringing a case in for a party unless you own a vineyard and are bringing your own label.

Servers (and some restaurant owners) prefer that tips be made with cash. The benefit to the restaurant is that they do not have to keep as much cash on hand if their policy is to tip out daily. The benefit to the servers is that they can take it with them and not wait for the next pay period.

It would also be interesting to get some consensus on what "generous" tipping is in the first place. No tip means the server must have been a complete idiot. 10% means the server did a poor job. 15% an average job, 20% thank you very much. But, I've also been told that if a server does an exceptional job 30% isn't beyond the pale. If they make the experience one you will never forget?? Thank them

Lastly, I absolutely HATE when gratuity is added to my bill. I am not a high school senior going to the prom handling my first check. I do not care how big the party is either. When gratuity is automatically added, I ask that it be removed. If it is not, I tip as outlined above maximum 15%. If they do remove it from the bill, I tip a minimum of 20% (including any alcohol). Lastly, there is no greater sin than to automatically calculate a gratuity and then bring a check to the table with a gratuity line as though it had not been added. How many servers are out there hoping the client does not notice and actually tips on the meal, the alcohol, the tax AND the pre-calculated tip? It is enough to make you never go back to such a place.

And as for Savoy? We never add a gratuity except to Savory Seminar attendees who have separate checks and include the gratuity in the fixed price and parties when requested. We appreciate that our clients expect great food paired with great wine and excellent service and therefore, will tip appropriately.

Admittedly, there are tax implications with tipping in cash that can be "preferential" to the server. This raises ethical issues. While I do not condone tax avoidance, I can say that most servers consider a tip of $10 in cash significantly better than the same amount on a credit card. Perhaps it is because they do not have to wait until their next paycheck, perhaps it is because they are not properly reporting. In the end the 'effective' tip is determined by the server's perceptions.

From Dave Baldwin:

Sorry, never been a waiter - but when I worked at Wendy's back in the day (circa 1995), I could tell you stories you would not believe about drive-thru customers. But, come to think of it, we had one guy come to the SuperBar (all you can eat buffet—they've gotten rid of it now) and pick up all the garlic rolls at one time with his bare hands, which were filthy and covered with axle grease. We had to throw them all away.

Then, he came back and did it again! We also had a guy come through the drive-through window drunk, and he passed out in his car. That ended up being quite a scene, especially since the manager thought he was dead.

From Kim Campbell:

A colleague who has traveled extensively—both domestically and internationally—said that a sure sign of a patron showing pretentiousness, but really not knowing what they're doing, is when they sniff the cork when a bottle of wine is served. True sommeliers never smell the cork—it does not tell anything about the wine's taste or quality.

From this same colleague (and supported by another colleague), patrons should never leave their napkin on the table when getting up to go to the restroom. They stated that proper etiquette is to leave the napkin on your seat or on the back of your chair because it is considered dirty and should not go back onto the table if it has been unfolded and used.

From me, when seated in a restaurant with booths, parents should never allow their small children to stand up and look over the back of the seat onto the table behind them. I usually smile and wave, but sometimes it gets tiresome if the child continues. Several of my thicker-skinned colleagues, who do not have children, said that they completely ignore the children instead of acknowledging them causing the kids to eventually turn around and sit down.

A colleague who has worked as a server before said that a warning sign is when patrons immediately ask her name, as if trying to get better acquainted. She said that it is always a warning light to waiters and waitresses that these patrons will bug the heck out of them and call them by name over and over and over.

You will have to bear with me, Sharon, because I am an editor and I work among a team of editors—we are all very exacting about proper use of language. One of my colleagues (the same one who has served tables before) stated that she hates it when the server returns to the table and says something like, "Are you still working on that?" instead of saying what they mean—"Have you finished your meal and may I take your plate?" She said that wording this request euphemistically forces the patron to respond in kind by saying, "Yes, I'm still working" or "No, I'm no longer working" or they have to back out of the figurative terminology and say, "Yes, I'm still eating." or "No, I'm no longer eating."

All of my team stated that they hated it when the server continuously returned to take plates because it puts the slowest eater under extreme pressure to hurry up if they are still eating and everyone else has already had their plates removed.

I feel it is rude (only my personal, yet humble, opinion) when passersby comment on, or even point at, food that has been ordered by another patron. Specifically, I have had the experience or observed others when a restaurant patron is seated in a restaurant, enjoying his or her selection. If the patron's table was located in the window of the restaurant or if the patron was seated outdoors in a cafe-like setting, I have observed others walking along the sidewalk, either outside of the restaurant or alongside the sidewalk cafe tables, pause to discuss or point at the food on the patron's plate.

Some have even asked the patron what he or she is eating. If I was being ushered to my table and I spotted something that had already been served to another patron that looked appealing, I would not point at it or bother the patron with questions. I would ask my server, "What type of salad is the patron in the red blouse at the table by the door having? It looks good."

From John Anderson:

I have a good friend of mine who drags me out to dine with him when he has to go with his mother-in-law. For the record, his mother-in-law is a drunk. OK let us be politically correct; she's an alcoholic, still a drunk in my book. We will arrive at the restaurant and if we have to wait for a table, she will wait at the bar. Red wine please. When we are finally seated, another wine. During appetizers, another one and of course, with the main course another.

Oh, I forgot to mention that before we left the house she had already had a few. The reason why my buddy invites me to these public displays of inebriation is: one, he's embarrassed and two, he married a woman who is just like her mother. That's another story. Back to the mother-in-law. As the mother-in-law gets progressively wasted, she starts to sneeze in rapid succession and blow her nose continually in the linen napkin.

Oh, I forgot to give you the restaurant setting. Fine dining, candles on the table, linen napkins and table setting, maître d, sommelier; you know the place. After she has deposited these precious bodily fluids in the white linen, she will call the waiter over to swap it out for a fresh napkin. Of course, by this time, all in the restaurant are aware of her and her loud nose and lousy hygiene; but a drunk never gets it nor is ever embarrassed.

From Cheryl McCadney:

I have friends who worked as waiters or waitresses in a variety of restaurant settings.

To the person, their experiences were the same whether they worked in a family restaurant or a highbrow white linen restaurant. Rude behavior has no color, ethnicity, gender, education level or economic-status preferences.

The shocking news (to me) was of the manner in which waiters/waitresses handled their special customers. It was common practice for waiters/waitresses to add "something extra" to the meals that they served when some customers chose to curse, scream, and threaten with physical violence during their restaurant visit. Use your imagination...

A common complaint among waiters/waitresses is that customers tip poorly. A waiter friend told the story of how a man came in with a date. He did everything to impress his date, i.e. ordering an expensive meal, bottle of vintage wine plus he made it a point to bark orders and talk down to the restaurant employees. At the end of the pricey meal, the man left a paltry tip and did so only after his female friend insisted that he leaves some sort of tip. Upon seeing the low tip, the waiter raced out to the parking lot to catch up with the man. At that time, he handed the man his tip back and stated, "Here, you left this behind. I have a feeling that you really need this more than I do."

From Kim Walker:

Always remember that servers are people too. Doesn't everyone deserve respect? Keep in mind that this is a job for them just as your job is for you. Some do this as a way to make extra money for Christmas or extra money for a vacation coming up, some do this as a way to put themselves through college (I held three jobs while I was in college - simultaneously - and two of them were wait-staff positions). Also, keep in mind that these servers could easily be your own children working their way through college or high school. Be respectful!

There is no room for "snooty" behavior - how about a quick, simple "thank you" when you are being served. I have had people give me the nastiest looks - as if I were their own personal slave or servant. It will not kill a person to smile at the server or give a quick thank you when he or she brings out the food. Even though you are "paying him" (with a tip) a simple gesture of kindness will not hurt. Besides, you have no idea of what the day has been like for your waiter. Maybe he has been on his feet for 7 hours instead of being home with his sick child.

The tip - oh my goodness - the tip. Here's my tip for you: Don't go out to eat if you cannot afford, or do not intend, to tip appropriately. Just do not do it! Many people are unaware that servers typically make less of an hourly wage than minimum wage. Why? Because the expectation is that the tips will make up the difference. When I was in college, I was paid a disgusting \$2.55/hour plus tips. That was when minimum wage was about \$5.15/hour. At another restaurant, I was only paid \$2.15/hour.

Enjoy your dinner!

My thanks to all the contributors for this section of *Don't be the Ugly Duckling at the Peacock Party: Why Waddle when You Can Strut?*

A Bit of Dining History

Ever wonder how some of the dining etiquette tips came to be? Here are some fun facts:

Table Linen

Before table linens were used as a sign of royalty, the poor people had no linens, or even tables. By the 12th century, the custom of using table linen was almost universal throughout France and Italy.

Napkins have been around since the Middle Ages when stylish folk stopped wiping their mouths on the tablecloth and started providing individual linen squares for themselves and their sloppier guests.

Silverware

Modern dining forks were invented in Italy. Thomos Coryat brought them to Europe in the 17th century. When Coryat showed the fork to his friends, they laughed at the new invention. However, only 50 years later people in England began to use forks.

Fingers are sure to be very useful for handing food, but they are blunt and they get sticky and dirty. Knives were the first pieces of cutlery. Some Stone Age wooden forks may date from as long ago as 7000 BC.

Dealing with Rude People

Mom used to say some people have no home training. That was her polite way of saying some people are downright rude and insufferable. For the sake of this book, I call them a type of ugly duckling. Let us explore how peacocks can handle them. Some of these suggestions are easier said than done, but remember you want to be better than they are.

If they brag or do something annoying, look at their facial expressions. Is their face blank and matter-of-fact, or does it have a smirk? If it is the latter, proceed on. If it is not, simply try to turn the conversation.

Take a second to maintain your calm. Breathe. After a while, you will start doing this automatically. Give a smart, although polite, reply that will not hurt either of you; but will deeply satisfy your feelings.

Here is an example:

"I only shop at the most elegant, high fashion, brand named stores. I love my Waterford stemware. What brand do you have?" You could say, "If I see something I like, I buy it. Congratulations on your Waterford. I am sure it is gorgeous."

On the other hand, your response could be a simple, "Good for you." Just leave it at that.

Always be on the ready. Whenever you are at leisure, think of some common uncomfortable comments or questions that people make, and make your own polite reply.

Do not give them what they want by acting jealous. If they keep bragging, just smile and say, "That's nice."

Demonstrate you are more mature than they are. Steer the conversation away to something they could not possibly be rude about, like the weather. Avoid them if they keep bothering you. Always, always,

always remember to keep your cool! Do not take anything that this person says seriously.

Keep a low voice when making replies; you want to make polite comments or questions, not ones that will get you in trouble. This will give the impression that you are much more mature, and therefore, will help you maintain your dignity.

Do not talk about them behind their backs. Remember, peacocks show maturity and respect for others.

Some people genuinely do not realize they are being rude. (Google: Asperger's syndrome) In case you have encountered someone like this, you may want to inform him or her politely that they have been rude. You will generally get an apology straight away. If not, it may just take patience!

It may take:

- Patience

- Common sense

- Snappy but polite comebacks

- Lots of people to back you up

And an extra set of clothes just in case they do something mean like spill food on you or dump water on you. Shame on them. Let your peacock civility and poise prevail.

Section 2. Workplace Etiquette

Ugly ducklings make the workplace unproductive and uncomfortable because of their lack of workplace etiquette. They wear too much cologne, gossip, have a negative attitude, show no respect for others' privacy and deadlines, and are constantly disruptive.

Peacocks not only focus on their performance goals, but also value the importance of teamwork and cooperation. By applying workplace etiquette, they accomplish a spirit of camaraderie that is necessary to succeed in the ever-stressful day-to-day operations of business. Even peacocks that work at home and rarely go into the office exude a polite and professional aura to their co-workers.

Cubicle Etiquette

Yelling across the office, loud music, competitive computer games, loud conversations and a brazen lack of basic cubicle etiquette in today's workplace have replaced what used to be a quiet, work-compatible atmosphere. So many American offices have been redesigned into cubicles, thus making cubicle etiquette a must for this home away from home environment.

Ugly ducklings are the ones who make all the noise that distract from having a productive workplace. They are rarely aware of their irritating behavior.

Peacocks, helpless victims of their loud ugly duckling co-workers, avoid the noisy disruption by popping in their iPod earphones (or other similar device) to soothe their frazzled nerves.

They also try to correct the situation by speaking calmly and directly to their ugly duckling co-workers about the need to concentrate on their work and asking politely if the ugly ducklings could find it in their hearts to 'turn down the volume.'

Workplace Gadget Etiquette Dos

Shut it off during Meetings

Unless you must use your PDA (Personal Digital Assistant) or cell phone during a meeting, presentation or other gathering, turn it off. Etiquette experts caution that whatever you gain in efficiency, you will likely lose in respect when your attention shifts from the meeting agenda to your gadget of choice. You have just announced that you are an ugly duckling.

When You Must Leave It On, Tell Others

Announcing to the group, "I'll text Angela for those figures," is a far cry from spending the entire meeting checking your email under the guise of efficiency.

Consider Your Audience and Environment

Acceptable gadget behavior at a technological startup in San Jose may be rude at an architectural firm in Philadelphia. Ugly ducklings will not impress anyone by wearing their iPods during a presentation or trotting out their IPhone over lunch. "If you're with a group that doesn't have your same level of technology adoption, they're not going to appreciate or be impressed by it," says Diane K. Danielson, coauthor of *Table Talk: The Savvy Girl's Alternative to Networking.*

Workplace Gadget Etiquette Don'ts

Ignore Cultural Differences

Remember: Boston is not Bangalore. Phillip Bergman, vice president of Roher Public Relations, says the Japanese have a "greater social consciousness" about cell phone use. "On public transit, they will cover their phones with their hands as they speak to keep the noise level down and maintain privacy. This is something I've adopted as a matter of courtesy and personal privacy."

Food in the Workplace Etiquette

Who has time to go out to eat lunch anymore? The demands of tight deadlines and mountains of work keep ugly ducklings and peacocks at their cubicles for lunch, usually warming food in the microwave.

Ugly ducklings (who care only about their wants and needs) are those who bring the smelly foods into their cubicles. Pleasant aroma to an ugly duckling can be nauseating stench to a peacock.

Peacocks are sensitive to powerful stinky foods and avoid them in the workplace. The odor permeates the entire floor and can be a distraction.

Be sensitive to other cultures. Foods from other cultures may have an unfamiliar aroma. Ugly ducklings criticize that which they do not understand. Peacocks may dislike the smell, but never embarrass or humiliate others.

Regardless of your cultural tastes, if your office has a mini-kitchen with a microwave oven, refrigerator, cabinets and sink, clean up after yourself. No one wants to see an ugly duckling's spilled or crusty food, dirty dishes, glasses and general gunk left for someone else to clean. This applies to your workspace, too. Keep it clean.

"Got a Minute?" Getting Rid of Intruders

How many times have you sat down in your cube to get work done, only to have an ugly duckling pop in for small talk? They want to talk about dribble that is important to them, but is of zero value to you.

Because ugly ducklings consider themselves the center of the universe, they have no regard for other people's time. They pop their heads into cubicles to gossip or talk about other matters of inconsequence. What does it matter to them that you are heads down entering information or diligently focused on an upcoming deadline? The ugly ducking wants to yak! To make matters worse, they can startle you out of your skin when they break your concentration.

Peacocks know there is a time and place for casual conversation. First, they make some sound of entry rather than barge into a cubicle. Peacocks ask, "Is this a good time?" When told it is not a good time, they politely leave the cubicle.

If you are the victim of the ugly duckling intruder, here are some tips to be in control of the situation:

- Tell them it is not a good time and that you will get back to them in a few hours, at lunch, later in the day, or tomorrow. Be firm and be sure to follow up.

- Post a DO NO DISTURB sign outside your office or cubicle. Be careful not to leave it posted all the time. It will lose its effectiveness and become meaningless.

- Put books on all your chairs. Intruders will have no place to sit.

- Visit the cubicle of the frequent offender before you start your focused work. Tell him or her you will be very busy for X hours and do not wish to be disturbed. Ask him or her help to keep people away from your cubicle.

Unwelcome Cubicle Décor

Ugly ducklings are oblivious to the discomfort to others caused by their hanging posters of swimsuit models, Chippendale dancers, half naked women, or political figures in their cubicles. Companies expect workers to decorate their home-away-from-home to make the space livable. However, if coworkers are offended by improper cubicle décor (and management does not address it), productivity and teamwork are negatively affected.

What would you do if you entered an office that had hair on the wall? Sound strange? I had an employee whose wife had extremely long luxurious hair. She was tired of having to take care of it and decided to cut it off. My employee was mortified because he worshipped her gorgeous locks. He gathered her fallen tresses, made it into a braid, brought it to the office, and pinned it to the wall next to his desk.

As they say in the South, his office mate had a "hissy fit" when he saw the hairy wall. He immediately ran to my office and announced that he could not work in an office with hair on the wall. I followed him to his office, saw the braid, called the lovesick husband into my office and explained why he had to remove the braid.

Clearly, it is critical that all employees work in a comfortable environment. The lesson is that the ugly ducking should ask management about the acceptability of questionable office décor. Peacocks always ask first or have a sense of proper décor.

Publicizing your Drama

The ugly duckling just got a call from his doctor with his test results. He calls his friends to share the news. Another ugly duckling just experienced a terrible break up with her boyfriend and just has to call all her girlfriends for support. Pity their cube mates or anyone within earshot of these conversations.

Peacocks avoid making personal calls from work, and keep their voices lowered when they do. If issues are deeply personal, go outside or to a private area and use your cell phone. People make judgments about your professionalism and your productivity based on the frequency and the etiquette with which you conduct private conversations.

Good Neighbors

Ugly ducklings can be annoying cubicle neighbors. They wear overly fragrant cologne or perfume, eavesdrop on neighbors' phone calls, sing aloud, blast music from online radio stations, etc.

Peacocks strive to create harmony and treat others the way they want to be treated.

Email Etiquette

Strutting and waddling are both visible indicators of poise or non-poise. Email offers another visual opportunity to demonstrate whether you are a peacock or an ugly duckling,

Look at the list that follows to determine if you are a peacock or an ugly duckling as it applies to your email etiquette:

Peacock (Strut)	Ugly duckling (Waddle)
Keeps emails concise and to the point	Writes emails requiring two or more page downs
Uses proper spelling, punctuation, and grammar	Rarely uses spell check. If using spell check, never verifies if it was 100% accurate
Rarely uses URGENT and IMPORTANT	Uses URGENT and IMPORTANT as often as possible to ensure recipient reads his email first
Rarely uses Return Receipt Request	Sends all messages with Return Receipt on, including mundane messages like "How was your evening?"
Uses lower case	USES UPPER CASE
Uses "Reply to Sender" frequently	Uses "Reply to All" frequently

Peacock (Strut)	Ugly duckling (Waddle)
Spells all words and avoids emoticons	Uses abbreviations and emoticons
Deletes chain letters	Forwards chain letters
Uses a meaningful subject	Omits including a subject or uses an unmeaning subject
Writes in short sentences	Writes with sentences that are ten words or longer
Writes or forwards emails that are professional and respectful	Writes or forwards emails containing racist, libelous, inflammatory, or obscene remarks
Deletes SPAM notes	Responds to SPAM
Uses cc: sparingly	Uses cc: liberally

Instant Messaging Etiquette

Instant messages, or IMs, allow coworkers to exchange information in real time. Yet IMs also present a way for ugly ducklings to waste time on involved personal conversations. Also, IM technology is not secure and, therefore, has the potential to leave corporate networks vulnerable to viruses and hackers. Therefore, while most companies are reluctant to eliminate instant messaging altogether, some have also been slow to embrace it and even slower to develop clear policies about its use, or misuse, in the workplace.

Instant Messaging Best Practices

Because many companies have yet to formalize rules of NETtiquette as it relates to IMs, an unsuspecting employee who uses instant messaging can wind up in hot water. Fortunately, some general standards and practices are beginning to govern the world of instant messaging. Here are some suggestions from workers who regularly use instant messaging at work:

Shut down Instant Messages when on conference calls. Meeting productivity comes to a halt if attendees are constantly responding to pings unless pings are directly related to the meeting.

Turn off your Instant Messages when giving presentations. A sure way to look like an ugly duckling is to have a personal message pop up on your screen during your presentation.

Do not hide behind Instant Messages. Do not let IMs rule the way you interact with people online vs. face-to-face. Be a peacock and continue nurturing those relationships.

Focus on what is important. Most ugly ducklings believe they can multitask: talk to a colleague, attend a phone call, and use IMs at the same time. You may well be able to do so, but do not let that distract you from the task at hand.

Be aware of other people's typing skills. You may be a fast typist, but that does not necessarily make others the same. Instead of pounding out six questions before the person on the other end has even answered the first, slow down.

When communicating with a Work-at-Home team member, realize they are working. There is no need to preface every message with "Are you there?" before calling.

Stay focused on business. Be careful sending personal messages. Imagine how embarrassing it would be if the receiver is conducting business with her boss looking over her shoulder at her screen and your IM pops up saying, "Have you seen Andre, the new guy? He is really a hottie!"

Avoid CAPS LOCK—the text equivalent of screaming. Just do not do it! You may be upset with something, maybe rightfully so, screaming does not guarantee results, and it builds resentment.

Easy on the acronyms. As mentioned in the email etiquette section, just because you may know what an acronym stands for does not necessarily mean everyone else does. Listen up, ugly ducklings. Too many acronyms remove the professionalism of the message.

Use Your "Away" Status Message. "If you just leave your portal open all the time, you can get distracted easily with the constant pop-ups. It can get very difficult to focus on the tasks at hand," says Jason Bergund, who relies on instant messaging to coordinate complicated activities between a suite of editing bays and their production teams for his job in New York City. "I custom-design my status messages to let people know when I'm busy, at lunch, on a phone call or working on a detailed document so they know that I'm busy without my having to respond to each and every instant-message query right in the moment."

Follow company policy. "Make sure you know your company's IM policies, if there are any," cautions Bergund. "Many companies, particularly companies in which large numbers of people in different locations have to coordinate their activities, understand that instant messaging is a great interoffice tool. But I've also worked at companies that really frowned on it." Find out if your company has applicable rules, and adhere to them. If a company policy doesn't exist, use common sense, and don't push the envelope.

Keep it professional. "Instant messages can get really lengthy, because they offer such an easy way to communicate," says Dana Bilbao, who works in production for a Los Angeles-based entertainment company. "Also, conversations have a tendency to get intimate very quickly because instant messaging can almost be like talking to you." Bilbao restricts her instant-messaging sessions to pertinent information, and she politely bows out when things start to get too personal.

Avoid discussing confidential information. "When you're instant messaging, always be aware that you're on an unsecured line," says Richie Fusco, an office manager for a securities firm in New York City. "I'm always careful not to discuss confidential or sensitive information over an instant message, because it's just too easy for pirates to hack into old conversation logs. And I always make sure that my virus and spy-ware protection is up to date."

Cell Phone Etiquette in the Workplace

Was there a time on this earth when cell phones were non-existent? Ugly ducklings treat their beloved cell phones as if they would perish without them. With the cell phones come behaviors that differentiate ugly ducklings from peacocks.

Following are tips to help ugly ducklings:

Keep your voice down. In a cube farm, there are no sound barriers. Take a walk either when your best friend calls or lower your voice.

Consider your office environment when choosing your ring tones. Be appropriate. You probably do not want coworkers to hear the ring tone version of "Baby's Got Back" every time you get a call.

Differentiate from your neighbor's ring tone. Change to avoid confusion whenever a neighbor's phone rings. This helps productivity for both of you, too.

Humor in the Workplace

Peacocks know that a sense of humor is a highly esteemed and admirable trait that demonstrates much of ones personality. A good laugh helps you relieve stress and gives you energy. Humor also brings people together during the workday and creates camaraderie that helps to break workplace tension.

Top management is wise to instill some humor into their corporate culture and allow a degree of levity to be included in their meetings and public image. As a peacock, do your part to be pleasant. Everyone enjoys being around those who are capable of an occasional smile now and then.

Jokes are a public x-ray of your true character. Listen carefully and people will tell you everything about their character through their jokes. All you have to do is tell a single joke that picks on any particular group of people and you will quickly find yourself to be considered an ugly duckling: one who is prejudiced, narrow-minded, racially, sexually, or ethnically biased. Much of today's humor is mean spirited and takes jabs at religious denominations, sexual or gender orientations, or nationality stereotypes.

Learn to tell at least three good jokes. Choose them wisely and practice timing and delivery with your family and friends before using them in public. Learn to tell your jokes with flair and end them properly with a well-rehearsed punch line. In case you are not a joke teller or the jokes you enjoy are not appropriate for the workplace, memorize a few humorous quotations to insert into conversations to illustrate your sense of humor.

Meeting Etiquette

When the ugly duckling leads a meeting, chaos reigns. The meeting can drag onward interminably without direction or purpose.

It wastes time, attendees are either bored or agitated, and the ugly-duckling leader of the meeting loses respect.

Techniques for Leading a Successful Business Meeting

Peacocks provide advance notice of the meeting to attendees. Everybody is busy; and because meetings require time and energy during a normal business day, advance notice is vital to ensure good attendance. Small, informal, inner-office meetings require less notice for attendance; but the peacock's associates will still appreciate as much prior notice as possible to arrange their schedules. If people from other departments are invited to a meeting, one week's notice is a thoughtful consideration. If people are coming from out of town, provide two weeks notice to allow attendees to make travel plans.

Immediately following the meeting, jot down brief notes regarding what occurred. If you wait too long, you might omit important details.

Soft drinks, coffee and snacks are a great enticement to lure people to your meetings. It is common today to see noted on some meeting announcement or agendas, "Refreshments will be served 15 minutes before the meeting." By announcing the availability of early refreshments, you are giving your attendees a chance to arrive prior to the meeting start time and prepare their snacks before the meeting starts.

If any guest in the meeting is unknown to the group, it is your role to introduce them to the group. If the meeting group is large (10 to 15 people), simply give the name of the guest to the group and do not take the time to make introductions and give the individual names of all the people in the room. However, if the unknown person is a client, a board member or a senior executive, give the name and title of each person in the room, if possible.

If people know one another, they do not need name tags. However, if there are important people in the room unknown to the group, as a courtesy to the guest, everyone should wear name tags to help that guest learn the names of those in the room. Since the majority of people are visual communicators, seeing a name in print helps them memorize the names in the room.

The best time of day to hold a meeting is 10:00 A.M. This mid-morning meeting time allows attendees to have time to stop by their offices, have a cup of coffee or tea, and check their phone and email messages. The least favorable time for meetings is Monday morning before 8:30 A.M. and Friday afternoon after 4:30 P.M. If a meeting involves a major decision that cannot be made in a brief time, it is unwise to plan a meeting too close to lunch when people are hungry and their blood sugar is low. They are more prone to being irritable.

Allow a quick break in a meeting if it lasts more than 70 minutes to give attendees the time they need to handle to their biological needs, check their phone or email messages, return any phone calls, get more coffee or socialize. Be considerate of the fact that business is still going on despite the importance of your meeting, and people need time to stay plugged into their routines and responsibilities.

Leave a few minutes for interaction during meetings, but be careful. Too much table talk among attendees can eat up meeting time and cause you easily to lose control. You may not be able to complete your agenda.

Peacocks reassure attendees (at least once during meeting) that they will do their best to end this meeting on time, as planned. This subtle reminder is one way to stay in control of the agenda.

Meetings are meant to be taken seriously. They are carefully designed to create a highly focused atmosphere suitable for conducting business. However, there is an obvious paradox at play because in the highly focused and serious atmosphere of the business meeting, peacocks are expected to use soft skills to participate. No wonder few people enjoy business meetings complaining that they are too frequent, too long and too boring. Even worse, too little gets accomplished. Using the above techniques will assist you in having a productive and meaningful business meeting.

Techniques for Attending a Business Meeting

To talk or not to talk? The mere fact meeting leaders invited you to attend their meeting indicates they believe you have a valuable contribution to make. Your role as an attendee is your opportunity to use your abilities at diplomacy, finesse and civility to make that contribution.

Ugly ducklings dominate a meeting with words of wisdom because of their vast experience (yeah, right!). Peacocks demonstrate poise and professionalism as a meeting attendee by applying the following tips.

Greet the meeting's leader (handshake optional) when entering the meeting. If you do choose to shake hands, remember your right hand should be dry and your handshake firm. Maintain eye contact and smile.

If you are a junior officer in the company, do not assume you can sit anywhere. Wait until others have taken their seats, or ask the meeting leader where they would like you to sit.

Avoid cross talk, whispering, or criticism during a meeting. No complaining is appropriate. You are there to create solutions.

Always put your attaché, man-bag or briefcase on the floor and never on the table. Women, use a purse hanger to keep your strapped purse both off the floor and off the table. Better yet, leave your purse in your office or cubicle, if possible.

"It is impossible to have a productive, interactive meeting with laptops separating the attendees. So, meeting participants should leave their laptops in their offices unless they have a reason to have them in the meeting," says Deborah Barrett, a senior lecturer at the Jones Graduate School of Management at Rice University. (That is, unless, of course, the meeting requires that users bring their laptops to follow along).

Be concise and participate during the meeting with informed contributions that add to the meeting, and do not ramble.

Stay on track and stick to the subject on the meeting's agenda.

Ugly ducklings resort to ranting on any subject. Peacocks remain optimistic and realistic on all subjects.

If a meeting starts at 9:00 and you arrive at 9:00, guess what? You are an ugly duckling because you are late. If you arrive at 8:50, you are a peacock because you are on time. Strive to arrive 10 minutes before a meeting's start time. This gives you time to talk to others and get yourself settled, allowing the meeting leader to start the meeting on time.

Show your total attention to those speaking by sitting up straight and focusing on them by giving them your direct eye contact.

Show up for the meeting prepared; and if you agree to a task during the meeting, keep your word and do it.

Smile. Appear pleasant and engaged in the meeting regardless of who is speaking, the topic, or the length of the meeting.

Do your homework ahead of time and know enough about the agenda and the topic to contribute to the meeting.

Take notes when appropriate. Ask questions to clarify any points of confusion.

Throw away any trash that accumulates during the break and after the meeting.

Thank the meeting leader after the meeting, handshake optional.

Cell Phone Etiquette During a Meeting

Because ugly ducklings consider themselves as the center of the universe, they see nothing wrong with taking a call on a cell phone during a meeting.

It is one thing to quickly hang up, apologizing to the meeting attendees; but quite another to continue the conversation, oblivious to the piercing and sharp glares from the meeting attendees.

Three possible locations to keep your phone are bag, belt or pocket. Many people choose to keep cell phones in their bags because of pocket-less wardrobes. If this is the case for you, be sure to choose a vibrating or single beep ring that is audible, yet minimal so it does not ring seven times while you search through your bag.

Ugly ducklings sit through an entire meeting wearing a Bluetooth, headset or any other hands-free-time-saving-quick-answer-annoying-accessory. Nonverbal communication speaks loudly. It accounts for 93% of communication. So, along with eye contact, smiling and open body language, involvement-shields, like the Bluetooth or cell phone headsets, can nonverbally send the wrong message; for example: "I am wearing this earpiece because I consider myself to be important and consider this meeting to be secondary to my many obligations."

A fool-proof solution to cell phone interruption is best personified by the words of Mr. Miyagi from The Karate Kid II, "The best way to block a punch is to not be there." In other words, just turn your phone off. This is a great way to avoid incoming calls or the temptation to make outgoing calls.

Keep your volume at a reasonable decibel level in an office setting. You will still hear it when you need to. If you are heading to a meeting and expecting an urgent call, fine—just put the phone where you can see or feel it when it rings, and let the meeting manager know you may have to take an urgent call.

Peacocks know the best time to check missed calls (their cell phones were politely silenced) is when they are away from the table. This will give them enough time to see what they missed, and if need be, return an emergency call. If they must return the call immediately, they do not do it at the table. They politely say, "Please excuse me for a minute, but I have to take this call."

Remember, you are always being watched. Poise and meeting etiquette are the professional's essential differentiators, especially when you are a meeting attendee.

Gadget Etiquette

Ugly ducklings live by the statement "whoever has the most toys wins the game." Technology produces new gadgets seemingly every six months. The ugly duckling has to have them. It is not a crime to have all the latest gadgets, but if they transform you into an ugly duckling, you will have problems.

We are lucky to live in the age of cell phones, personal digital assistant's (PDAs) and other electronic helpers—all small enough to tootle around with us all the time. Too many folks have become tethered to their techie toys (particularly men), who like to have their gear within easy reach and cannot be bothered with retooling their look when they leave the office. It is understandable if you have a tech-heavy position, like the support desk where you need to be ready; or are a firefighter with tools dangling from every belt loop; or happen to be a superhero like Batman with 50 lbs. of gadgets needed to save the world.

Nevertheless, as soon as you start socializing with work colleagues, you need to make a switch out of your Batman "uniform." Store your headsets and Bluetooth earpieces in your pocket or your laptop case. As long as you wear the clip-on holster for your Blackberry to one side (more hidden) and on your natural waistline (not sagging under your gut), you will look polished, rather than resembling Mr. Fix-It. After hours, try to limit yourself to one gadget on your belt.

"Meanwhile, too many of us have lost all sense of decorum," says Teri Agins, fashion reporter. "It's rude, and looks uncool, to keep glancing down, fidgeting, text-messaging and monitoring email. Be an attentive guest and shut off your devices for a while. You'll be forced to tune into the world that surrounds you."

Telephone Etiquette

People who otherwise mind their manners commonly make telephone errors. In personal calls, the following actions qualify as ugly duckling etiquette missteps. For business calls they can make you look unprofessional.

Conversing with someone nearby while your phone mate is on the line is permissible only when a third party's participation is necessary or you acknowledge it by saying something like, "I hope you don't mind if I quickly ask Diane what she thinks about this."

Typing, washing dishes, or shuffling papers while on the telephone suggest that your attention is elsewhere.

Texting When You Should Be Talking

Typing rather than talking will not win you any etiquette bonus points. Text messaging, in particular, can be viewed as an intrusion. "It's one thing if you discuss something important and say, 'Give me a second. I want to send myself an email before I forget what we've just discussed,' and then quickly use your Blackberry or PDA. Then, put it away," says Leah Ingram, author of *The Everything Etiquette Book*. "It's an entirely different thing to be on your Blackberry and not fully paying attention when someone else is giving a presentation, especially if this goes on for the entire meeting." Text messaging "forces you to lose eye contact and sends the message that you're not fully engaged," says Joseph Sommerville, president of Peak Communication Performance and coauthor of the "Business Etiquette: Manners Mean Business" audio program.

A major etiquette blunder is to use a hands-free telephone to conduct a phone call while you eat your lunch. Eating while on the telephone is not only impolite, but is seen by many as crude.

I confess this next one is like fingernails on a blackboard to me. Hearing the smacks of a gum chewer may not annoy everyone, but many will take offense. To be on the safe side, save the gum for later.

If you have to sneeze, cough, or blow your nose, either turn your head away or excuse yourself for a moment and put the receiver down. If possible, hit the mute button.

You know gadget-related behavioral excesses have gotten out of hand when etiquette columnists tackle text messaging and PDAs.

For example, here is an excerpt from the syndicated "Ask Thelma" etiquette column, written by Thelma Domenici: "The etiquette of technology doesn't deviate from etiquette standards we all know. Etiquette and manners are about thinking of others before us and treating them with respect and courtesy in all our actions—even those dominated by technology."

But techies who regularly hold the door and remember to send thank-you notes don't always know when to turn off their cell phones. In a Robert Half Technology survey, 67 percent of 1,400 CIOs (Chief Information Officer) queried said breaches of technology etiquette are increasing.

With such concerns in mind and a polite nod to varying job requirements, here is a peacock guideline for minding your tech-gadget manners as you manage your career:

Admit You Are a Gadget Freak

Ugly ducking tech enthusiasts may be oblivious to their faux pas. "I think that the zealots are quite possibly the least likely to honor standard rules of etiquette, in my experience, because they seem to think that those on the other end of a digital connection are just as important -- or even more so -- than those who they're with face-to-face," says technology guru Dave Taylor. "Just remember that except in extraordinary situations, the person you're facing should take precedence over the person you're IMing, SMSing or even chatting with on your latest device."

Death of a Co-worker in the Workplace

If someone in your office dies, or the family member of an associate dies, a peacock shows respect by sending condolences. Gestures of sympathy help them and the family's loved ones process the grief that arises during this time.

Ugly ducklings feel awkward at these sensitive times and avoid the bereaved or say something that is inappropriate. Peacocks show respect by knowing rules of handling a topic that can be uncomfortable.

Every religion and culture has its own acceptable funeral rituals according to the faith of its practitioners. If you do not know how to honor the loss of a business associate, contact the funeral home, the deceased's house of worship or ask a family member for their guidance about ways you can show your respect. Many religious faiths do not want you to send a gift of flowers, but instead, they prefer to receive consolation gifts of vegetarian food. Some faiths prefer cash donations be given to the remaining family of the deceased.

Here are some suggestions for dealing with the death of a close business associate:

You read about a close business associate's death in the obituary section of your local newspaper. The obituary will tell you if the services will be held for those who would like to pay their respects to the family of the deceased, or whether there will only be private services for the family only.

The obituary may also give instructions for those who want to express their sympathy. For example, a comment may say, "The family asks that in lieu of flowers, a donation be made to____ (a charity, church, medical research association)," or "Flowers may be sent to the Sycamore Street Funeral Home," or "Flowers may be sent to the Lincoln Cemetery."

Coworkers will generally send a gesture of sympathy as a group, company or department. Appropriate arrangements for the service could be a standing spray, standing basket or fireside basket.

Send sympathy cards to the family of the deceased. Send simple non-religious cards unless you are sure of the religious faith of the deceased's family. Many people at your office may sign the card.

When sending a card to a widow, address the card using her formal married name. For example, write Mrs. Reginald Flores rather than Mrs. Gertrude Flores, Ms. Gertrude Flores, or Gertrude Flores.

If you hear about the death of your associate at the office, ask the person who gave you information about the funeral services. If they do not have the information, help arrange for someone to call the family and identify himself or herself as a work associate. The person calling should tell the family member they are calling to inquire about the funeral arrangements. They should express their sympathy to the person who answers the phone.

When you attend the funeral, the family is preoccupied with their thoughts about their loss and cannot hear the words you say to them. Express very simple, yet emotional condolences, such as, "I will miss her," or "John was my friend," or "My sympathy."

Do not be afraid to mention the deceased employee's name at work. Everyone grieves in his or her own way and communication lessens the sadness. However, if the grief persists, seek professional help.

Grief in the Workplace

If the deceased is a spouse or close relative of a co-worker, you may choose to attend the services together or individually. If you are attending the services, offer your condolences to your coworker but do not bring up issues surrounding work. Offer your support and understanding over their loss. Once a coworker returns to work, you may wish to extend your support and sympathy, but remember to respect their privacy if they do not wish to discuss their loss.

Management Support

Recovery of your work group depends (to a great extent) on the effectiveness of the grief leadership provided by you, the group's manager or owner of the company. Effective peacock grief leadership guides members of the work group as they mourn and memorialize the dead, help their families, and return to effective performance of their duties.

Consider providing a private area were co-workers can mourn without public scrutiny. Initially, close friends and associates will feel shock and intense grief. If the loss is to be resolved, it is essential for all affected employees to spend time talking about the deceased person, sharing memories, and discussing the loss. This "grief work," which is essential for recovery, is intensely painful when done alone, but much less so when it can be shared with friends. Providing a private area where co-workers can talk together and shed tears without public scrutiny will ease this process.

Get back to the work routine in a way that shows respect for the deceased. Returning to the work routine can facilitate healing if the work group makes an effort to uphold values held by the deceased and strive toward goals that he or she particularly valued, for example, "I want to show the customers I care, because Rebecca was such a caring person."

Finally, do not treat a new employee like a "replacement" for the employee who died. It is important that new employees not be made to feel like "replacements" for employees who have died. Reorganizing responsibilities and moving furniture can help spare everyone the painful experience of having somebody new at "Deidre's desk" doing "Deidre's job."

My friend, Wendi Brooks-Lester offers another suggestion for co-workers mourning the death of a loved one. If possible, send notes and cards to people's residences instead of leaving them on a person's desk. That way it will be easier for the person to focus on work items while at work.

I hope you never have to endure the grief mentioned in this topic. If you do, use these tips to display your poise and professionalism, even during times of profound sadness.

Religious Sensitivity in the Workplace

Ugly ducklings assume that their religious practices (or lack thereof) are the only way one should worship. The peacock demonstrates sensitivity by keeping an open mind and asking questions.

If coworkers dress in religious clothing or pray during the business day, ask them to explain their religion; including the significance of their clothing and their prayer customs. Ugly ducklings create prejudice and fear by being ignorant of other people's customs.

If you practice your own religious customs in the workplace, do not use your company's supplies, equipment or company time to spread the word about your own personal beliefs.

If you pray often during the day because of your religious customs, make up for that time with your employer by coming in early or staying late.

Avoid practicing religious bias by commenting on other beliefs. Avoid discussions about religion that are contentious or preachy. Avoid any humor that demeans people's religious faith.

Peacocks respect other people's religious holidays. If you do not understand the significance of those holidays, ask. You strengthen relationships and respect by coming together.

Finally, when planning holiday parties in the workplace, consider playing non-religious music and serve a variety of foods that include vegetarian and kosher dishes. Offer non-alcoholic beverages for those who do not drink alcohol.

Section 3. Miscellaneous Etiquette Tips

Life tosses circumstances daily to both ugly ducklings and peacocks requiring them to demonstrate sensitivity to the situation. The ugly ducklings fail because they are uneasy when caught outside of their comfort zone or have not taken the time to know that etiquette applies to so many broad events. The peacocks handle these situations with ease and comfort because they know how to show respect and proper etiquette to all.

Events such as dealing with the hard of hearing or the blind can be uncomfortable to those who want to be sensitive but do not know how. They risk going too far to make everyone comfortable and end up patronizing.

On the other hand, every day events such as riding an elevator, escalator, or standing on a moving sidewalk seem quite senseless, requiring no thought. However, there are etiquette rules even for these simple events. The peacocks who know the rules demonstrate the poise and professionalism that sets them apart from the ugly ducklings.

We have all been to weddings, funerals, etc. These are also life events requiring etiquette awareness.

Etiquette for People Who Are Hard of Hearing

Have you had an occasion to talk to someone who is hard of hearing or deaf? How did you handle it? Did you talk louder or even YELL to make you heard? If you did, guess what? You are ugly duckling who has diminished an opportunity for a meaningful and respectful communication with that person.

My friend, Burton King, a specialist in the field of hearing suggested that this book include etiquette for interacting with hard of hearing people.

Here are some facts and interaction tips to ensure you are always a peacock, demonstrating professionalism and sensitivity to a person who is hard of hearing.

People who are deaf or hard of hearing have a unique culture. They communicate with a language that people with normal hearing may not understand.

People who are deaf or hard of hearing generally prefer to communicate orally. The deaf and hard of hearing may not have 100% hearing loss, and can use residual sound when communicating. Phonetically their speech is correct even though their pitch and tone may sound different than what a normal hearing person is used to.

Some deaf and hard of hearing people learn American Sign Language (ASL) to make communicating with others quicker and easier. Some who are deaf and hard of hearing, especially people who became deaf as an adult, often adapt a communication style that is a combination of oral, lip reading and sign language.

There are a wide range of hearing losses and communication preferences. If you do not know the individual has a preferred communication method, ask! Do not assume. If you are able, use the style that they use (i.e., sign, oral, etc.)

If you experience extreme difficulty in communicating orally, ask if writing is all right. Never say, "Oh, forget it, it is not important." A conversation can be held with two people sharing a keyboard and the view of a computer screen. Many deaf individuals may or may not be highly proficient in English. Spanish or French (for example) may be their first language. Assume their English skills are strong, but be willing to make adaptations if they are not.

Be normal. Make direct eye contact. Natural facial expressions and gestures will provide important information to your conversation.

Do not shout or exaggerate your speech. It does not help communication, so talk as you normally would. Keep your face and mouth visible by not obscuring them with your hands, hair, or food. While you are speaking, you should look at the listener's face and smile with encouragement and assurance, as needed.

When speaking to a person who lip-reads, speak clearly and evenly. Peacocks never over-articulate. Provide an occasional brief period of silence between statements. The listener may wish to respond or think through what has been said. Use transitional phrases between topics, such as "My next question is about…" or "Okay, I'm going to change the subject." Changing the topic abruptly can cause confusion. Tell your story completely and end it before changing to another subject. If you are talking and asked to repeat yourself several times, try rephrasing your sentence. To get a person's attention, call his name. If there is no response, lightly touch him on the arm or shoulder.

If you do not understand what they are saying, do not pretend to understand. Ask them to repeat what they are saying.

The deaf or hard of hearing person may have an interpreter. This person generally should not be included in the conversation. If the deaf or hard of hearing individual is a speaker for an event, the interpreter commonly stands at his or her side. If the person has an interpreter, address questions, comments or concerns directly to the individual, rather than the interpreter.

When giving a number or an address, consider alternative ways to provide it: writing, faxing, or e-mailing are great ways to ensure accuracy. Consider the environment where you are talking. Overly bright or dark places can be a barrier to clear communication. Good lighting is important, but keep in mind the glare factor and do not stand in front of a sunny window. Control or eliminate competing environmental noise that could cancel out or interrupt speech.

If at an event, seat the deaf and hard of hearing in the front of the room with a good view of the speaker so that they can read lips, see gestures and take notes of sounds they can make out.

My friend, Lee Holliday, who is hard of hearing, adds the following advice:

Nearly deaf or hard of hearing individuals have a more narrow range in which they hear comfortably than those who hear normally. If the volume is too low, the speaker may not even be heard or the words will sound just like a mumble. On the other hand, if the volume is too high, it hurts their ears and they cannot focus on what is being said because of the discomfort.

Lee suggests we should speak a little slower, but not so slow that it sounds over-exaggerated and patronizing.

Finally, he says it is more difficult for the hard of hearing to understand unfamiliar accents, so it is especially important to pay close attention to proper enunciation and speaking at a desirable volume and pace.

Etiquette for the Blind

According to the American Federation for the Blind, "etiquette" may seem a rather formal term to describe the give and take of our interactions with friends and family; but it really is just another way of describing the thoughtful, considerate behavior that peacocks expect to receive from others and give to them.

Until a friend or relative becomes visually impaired, you may never have known anyone who could not see well, or not at all. Therefore, you had no reason, or at least no immediate need, to think about the subtle differences between considerate behavior toward a sighted person and someone with limited vision.

These are not major differences—the same affection, politeness and thoughtfulness apply—but there are several basic ground rules that will make your day-to-day contacts with a friend or relative who is visually impaired easier, more relaxed, and truly helpful. This section outlines the key points to keep in mind when you are with someone whose vision is impaired, including:

- Acting as a sighted guide

- Respecting the person's ability to do things for himself or herself

- Giving directions

- Speaking directly

- Maintaining a conversation

Tact and Courtesy

If you feel like you are an ugly duckling because of any uncertainty about what is and is not courteous, tactful behavior toward a friend, relative, or complete stranger who is blind or visually impaired, here are suggested guidelines. Keep in mind that, in the case of someone you are close to, it is entirely possible to continue having a mutually rewarding, supportive relationship; to have relaxed, spontaneous discussions; and to enjoy most, if not all, of the activities you shared in the past.

Feel free to use words that refer to vision during the course of a conversation. Vision-oriented words such as look, see, and watching TV are a part of everyday verbal communication. The words blind and visually impaired are also acceptable in conversation.

Be precise and thorough when you describe people, places, or things to someone who is very blind. Do not leave out things or change a description because you think it is unimportant or unpleasant.

It is perfectly acceptable to refer to colors, patterns, designs, and shapes.

When you speak about someone with a disability, refer to the person and then to the disability. For example, refer to "a person who is blind" rather than to "a blind person."

If a friend, relative, or stranger on the street is traveling with a dog guide, do not pet the dog, offer it food, or distract it in any way while it is working. Dog guides are not pets. They are highly trained mobility tools.

If you see someone who is blind, or visually impaired, about to encounter a dangerous situation, be calm and clear about warning the person. For example, if he or she is about to bump into a luggage cart in a hotel lobby, calmly and clearly call out, "Wait there for a moment; there is a luggage cart in front of you."

Do not take care of tasks for the person that he or she would normally do, such as change television channels, cut meat, or salt and pepper food. First, ask if the person needs help, then offer to assist. Most people with a visual impairment will tell you if they would like some assistance.

If you are asked to complete a task for someone, always leave things in the same place you found them.

Do not move furniture or other articles in your friend's home or your own home without letting the person know.

Communicating Comfortably

While most people who are visually impaired have some vision, peacocks never assume that their friend or relative can make out where they are and what they are doing in the same room.

When greeting a friend who is blind or visually impaired, do not forget to identify yourself. For example, "Hi, Jane, it's Quincy."

Speak directly to your friend or relative who is visually impaired, not through an intermediary.

Speak distinctly, using a natural conversational tone and speed. Unless the person has a hearing impairment, you do not need to raise your voice.

Address your friend or relative by name, so he will immediately know that you are talking to him rather than someone who happens to be nearby.

As soon as a friend, relative, or stranger who is blind or visually impaired enters a room, be sure to greet the person by name. This alerts her to your presence, avoids startling her, and eliminates uncomfortable silences.

Be an active listener. Give the person opportunities to talk. Respond with questions and comments to keep the conversation going. A person who is visually impaired cannot necessarily see the look of interest on your face, so give verbal cues to let him or her know that you are actively listening.

Always answer questions and be specific or descriptive in your responses.

Say when you are leaving and where you are going if appropriate. For example, "I'm going to the kitchen to get a drink of water."

Indicate the end of a conversation with a person who is completely blind or severely visually impaired to avoid the embarrassment of leaving the person speaking when no one is actually there.

Wedding Etiquette

I confess I am shocked at some of the ugly duckling behaviors regarding weddings that friends have mentioned to me. Take the following dos and don'ts to heart. They come from Sabrina Torti, founder of Proposing Dreams wedding planners of Kirkwood and Collinsville, Missouri.

- Do RSVP as soon as possible: definitely RSVP by the due date.

- Do call as soon as possible if you must change your plans after accepting the invitation.

- Do only bring guests listed on the invitation. Be sure to ask if you can bring someone other than those listed. If yours is the only name on the invitation, do not bring a guest.

- Do arrive on time.

- Do consider taking pictures at the reception to share with the couple.

- Do be sure to thank the couple before you leave and tell them what a great time you had.

- Do watch your alcohol consumption. Respect the occasion and stay within your limits.

- Do not take children to a wedding without making sure they are invited, rested and supplied with snacks, entertainment and supervision.

- Do not leave your cell phone on during the ceremony.

- Do not take your gift to the wedding or reception. (I know we ALL do it.) It can be a headache for the couple or their family to get it home. If possible, have the gift mailed. You can even send it after the wedding.

Symphony Etiquette: Rookie's Guide to the North Carolina Symphony

Peacocks and ugly ducklings can appreciate the joy of hearing a lovely symphony, piano or violin soloist. The peacock knows and practices the etiquette for such elegant matinee and evening performances. However, without this knowledge, ugly ducklings may be in a quandary about how to handle themselves at such prestige performances.

The North Carolina Symphony is an American orchestra based in Raleigh, North Carolina, with sixty-nine full time musicians. Jeannie Mellinger is the Director of Public Relations for the North Carolina Symphony and offers the following etiquette section to make the entire visit to a symphony an enjoyable experience. Although Ms. Mellinger focuses on the North Carolina Symphony, this advice applies to symphony halls around the world.

Basic Survival Level:

What should I wear?

Always obey our rule: be comfortable. You will see a range of dress—some concertgoers are weekend casual while a few others may raise the bar with formal suits and gowns. However, by a long country mile, most patrons dress in some version of business casual: a suit or sport coat for men, a dress or nice pants for women.

What happens if I am late?

In deference to your fellow concert-goers, you won't be seated while the orchestra is playing. Ushers will show you to your seat at the completion of a movement or work.

Can I bring my kids?

Yes, we welcome children who can sit quietly for a two-hour concert. Tickets for children 11 and under are $5. A word to the wise: children, no matter how lap-friendly, will need a ticket.

Is there any food or drink available at the hall?

The City of Raleigh operates two snack bars in the Meymandi Concert Hall lobby. Wine, beer, water and soft drinks are available as well as cookies, candy and treats of that sort. However, unlike at the movies, you may not bring these items into the hall. Music feeds the soul, so you will be fine.

When should I clap?

Look around. Find a distinguished-looking individual, maybe the one who avidly reads the program notes before the concert or shushes people who are whispering. When this person begins to clap, you can too.

Musicology 101:

Why are there numbers at the end of the titles of works? And what do the letters mean?

Originally, the opus (abbreviated as op. and meaning "work") number was assigned by the composer or publisher. Because everyone used a different system to assign opus numbers, they were unreliable. Scholars began to create catalogues of the works of individual composers.

As an example, the works of Johann Sebastian Bach were catalogued by Wolfgang Schmieder in 1950. The catalogue number is indicated by the letters BMV, Bach Werke Verzeichnis or Bach Works Catalogue. The catalogue is arranged thematically—by genre—instead of chronologically. The choral works are listed first, then organ works, other keyboard works and so on.

Why are the musicians seated they way they are?

Tradition. Any conductor can direct any orchestra and know almost exactly where musicians will be seated. Imagine the disaster created by a conductor trying to signal the brass to come in only to discover he is cueing the piccolos. Sections are always seated together to ensure that members can hear their colleagues clearly.

The more melodic instruments are placed near the front of the stage to emphasize that part of the music. Even though they are fun to watch (drums, chimes, bells, blocks, cymbals and that snappy thing!), the percussionists are the least melodic and are placed at the back of the stage. Also, the strings do not project as much as the percussion and brass instruments do and would be difficult to hear if those louder instruments were placed in front of them.

What is the difference between a concerto and a symphony?

The concerto and the symphony are the two most commonly heard types of works orchestra programs. They are both multi-movement compositions—usually four movements for a symphony and three for a concerto. The most obvious difference is that the concerto features a soloist. In concertos, there is usually a moment for the soloist to show off virtuoso technical skills, and even improvisational skills, called the cadenza. Most often, this moment occurs near the end of the first movement.

An Italian lesson, please. What do all these terms mean?

Adagio: Slowly, leisurely

Allegro affettuoso: Lively, with passion

Andante, ma non troppo lento: Moderately slow, but not too slow

Appassionato: With passion

Canzone: A song

Calzone: An <u>Italian</u> <u>turnover</u> made from <u>pizza</u> dough and stuffed with cheese

Con tonno: With tuna

Canzone con tonno: A song with tuna

Piano: Well, yes, it's a keyboard instrument, but as a musical direction it means "softly."

Vivace: Lively, animated, brisk

Tips for All:

- Try very hard to cough only between movements. If this is completely impossible, it is really better to slightly inconvenience your aisle-mates by getting up and leaving the hall until the fit passes than to continue coughing and disturbing everyone around you. They will thank you.

- If you have a cold/cough, please bring cough drops and use them. Unwrap the paper or foil before the concert starts.

- Please consider your fellow concertgoers—leave the jangly bracelets and strong perfume or aftershave for another night.

- Secure your program books. When a program book hits the ground, it can sound like a shotgun blast, especially during a quiet movement.

- Turn off cell phones and pagers and do not even **think** about taking pictures or using recording devices. Also, it is bad form to hold up Bic lighters, even if you mean it as a compliment.

- Check your calendar to make sure you are coming on the correct night.

- Give yourself plenty of time to arrive, park, walk, use the restroom and so on. You do not want to spend the first ten minutes of the concert gasping for breath.

- Visit our website to get information ahead of time; plan to try out some of our pre- and post concert events. Go to www.ncsymphony.org for tips on planning your visit to a symphony. Also, check the website in the case of inclement weather for up-to-the-minute information on delays or postponements. For those visiting the North Carolina Symphony, you will find the latest uPersonal Digital Assistanttes on the left side of the home page under "What's New."

- Did you have a good time? Tell your friends!

Cruise Etiquette Tips

A cruise is unlike any other vacation and you have worked towards it for a number of months or even years. A cruise will provide you with relief from the rigors of daily life. It gives you a sense of freedom from daily commitments, schedules, appointments and mandatory events that one must attend. Nothing can put a damper on a cruise vacation quicker than ugly ducklings who have left their manners at home. It is proper to have a sense of shipboard etiquette, good manners and common courtesies toward fellow passengers while aboard a cruise. The following are some suggestions on how ugly ducklings can become peacocks while enjoying their freedom from their normal daily routine.

Dress Properly and Adhere to the Shipboard Dress Code

During your process of selecting a cruise vacation, notice what type of dress atmosphere the cruise line is offering in its brochure. Cruise documents are on their internet site so you should not have any surprises when you arrive onboard. Most cruise lines are resort casual by day and more formal by night. The cruise staff will advise you via the daily onboard newsletter and other means as to what the dress code will be for the main restaurant on any given day. Many cruise lines now have alternate dining facilities that are usually casual attire. Dress accordingly to what has been published and at the appropriate times. If it is a formal night, ladies should wear a cocktail dress or a gown, gentlemen should wear a tuxedo or dark suit. If it is informal, ladies should wear a cocktail dress or dressy pantsuit or similar, gentlemen should wear a jacket and tie. If it is casual, ladies should wear skirt or slacks with a blouse or sweater, gentlemen should wear slacks and a shirt and/or a sweater.

Casual does not mean showing up in your warm-ups, cut off shorts or a tatty pair of old jeans for the evening. Recently some ugly ducklings have taken to changing back into casual clothes after a formal or informal diner. This does not create a good atmosphere, nor is it pleasant to many people who cruise and look forward to enjoying the formal and informal evenings aboard ship.

Holiday Party Etiquette

When invited to someone's home, peacocks know to take a gift for the host. Ideally, you should do some homework to make your gift unique and meaningful. Flowers and wine are common gifts and others may appear at the door with them. As an example, stand out by providing the host with exotic coffee or tea along with a funky coffee cup or teapot. Do they prefer caffeinated or decaffeinated? Better find out first.

The alcohol will flow freely. People are watching you! Get drunk and you can be sure they will be consider you a lush. Folks may laugh with you, slap you on the back, and make off-color jokes. After the sun rises the next morning and they reflect on the holiday party and how you acted, do you think they will want to invest their money into you (now the ugly duckling) and your business? The secret is to have a glass in your left hand throughout the party and nurse whatever you are drinking. Teetotalers should stick with their soft drinks, water, and iced tea. Those preferring alcohol can enjoy their drinks, but keep drinking in moderation by drinking no more than two or three drinks maximum. Before leaving the party, switch to coffee or water to make sure you are able to drive.

Practice your positive handshake, eye contact, and small talk techniques at the party. Approach strangers and get them to talk about themselves. People love to talk about themselves. They will appreciate you more for listening to them. You should be talking 20% of the time and listening 80% of the time. You are listening for cues as to whether folks can be potential new friends or customers for your product or service. Contact them after the holidays as a follow up. For more on these tips, refer to my book *Wild Woman's Guide to Etiquette: Saving the World One Handshake at a Time*, available on www.amazon.com.

Open yourself up to diversity. Observe the Christian Christmas, the Jewish Rosh Hashanah, African American Kwanzaa, and any other events that are different from your own. (Note: Do not assume all African-Americans celebrate Kwanzaa. Ask before assuming.) You open yourself up to an untapped source of new acquaintances and customers.

Be respectful of new customs. Imagine how others will hold you in high esteem for sharing this special time with them.

Enjoy the food, but do not be an ugly duckling and pig out. You need your hands free to shake hands. If you are walking around a holiday event with a plate full of food, you are derailing an opportunity to meet others in a professional manner. Some of the more first-class events have wait staff walking around the rooms offering delicious hors' doeuvres, such as mini crab cakes, spanakopita (pastry stuffed with spinach), stuffed mushrooms, etc. Take two or three from the tray, place them in your napkin, eat and toss your napkin in the proper disposal.

Occasionally, check your teeth in the washroom to ensure you do not have food particles stuck between your teeth. You can be sure that if you have food in your teeth while trying to discuss your business, folks are looking at your teeth and not hearing a word you say. Avoid garlic dishes or any food that will make your breath stink. Potential customers or friends will be trying to find ways to get away from you rather than suffer through your bad breath.

Finally, be sure to send a thank you note or card to your hosts after the event. This demonstrates you are a peacock with poise and knowledge of basic etiquette.

Perils of the Office Holiday Party

Your company's holiday gathering is just around the corner—time to let loose and party with your coworkers after a long year, right? Wrong.

According to business etiquette expert Hilka Klinkenberg, the cardinal rule is to remember that no matter how festive the occasion, it is still about business. Do not fall off the fast track to success or risk damaging your professional reputation in one night of inadvertent blunders. Klinkenberg offers the following advice to ensure a smooth, enjoyable evening.

Eat, drink and be merry in moderation. Where else but the office party can you find the CEO and the mailroom clerk bellied up to the bar together? But remember: Alcohol plus you and your boss can equal Monday morning's "I can't believe I said that." If you choose to drink, do so minimally.

Dress appropriately for the occasion. Klinkenberg says this rule especially applies to women who sometimes use company parties to strut their stuff. Peacocks leave anything short, tight or revealing in the closet. You have worked hard to create a professional image, and revealing clothes can alter your coworkers' and manager's perception of you as a competent professional.

Your company party may be the only time you see the president, CEO or VPs in person. Introduce yourself. This is a great opportunity to become visible to your organization's higher-ups. At the very least, do not spend the entire evening with your regular office buddies. Get in the holiday spirit and mingle with people from other departments.

Find out who can come to the event. Spouses and significant others are not always on the guest list. Check beforehand to avoid a potentially uncomfortable evening.

If you have been a star performer in your organization, you may be honored with a toast. Accept the honor gracefully, but do not drink to yourself or clap when others are applauding you. Also, make a toast to the person who toasted you, thanking him for the recognition.

Pay attention to the time you arrive and when you leave. Even if you do not really want to attend, avoid arriving 20 minutes before the end just to make an appearance. On the other side, do not party into the wee hours either. Coworkers and managers will notice both errors in judgment.

Be sure to thank those who coordinated the party. They likely put in a great deal of effort hoping you would have a good time. Not only is saying thank you the nice thing to do, but it also makes you stand out from the many employees who do not.

If you are in charge of planning the party, a few reminders:

Consider your employees' diversity. A Christmas party may alienate some staff. A holiday party is more inclusive.

Is a daytime or evening party more convenient for attendees? For employees with children, arranging childcare for an evening event may be an issue. If you plan a party during office hours, however, make sure everyone can attend.

Clearly convey to employees who is invited to the party. If spouses or children are not included, say so.

Plan an event that reflects well on the company. Choose an appropriate location, control the alcohol flow, and consider your employees' interests.

Regifting Etiquette

Regifting means giving a gift that was given to you to someone else, yet acting as if you bought it especially for your recipient. Sure, you saved money, but be careful. What if your recipient finds out you have regifted? Will that person put you into the ugly duckling category?

The best approach is to be upfront when regifting, but why spoil the moment? If you tell your mother-in-law, "I have no use for this cheap watch, so I'm giving it to you," even a person in need of a watch will hate you. Be a peacock and say nothing to avoid problems.

To avoid being labeled as a regifter, follow these rules:

Do update the wrapping. The next most common regifting faux pas, after leaving the previous gift card attached, is to regift in the original, now crinkled and possibly torn wrapping paper or box. If the phrase "Hey, it looks almost new" crosses your desperate ugly duckling brain, remember that the "almost" is a dead giveaway to the new recipient.

Do not give hand-me-downs as regifts. Novice regifters (and those who are terminally ugly ducklings) often get these two categories confused. A hand-me-down is an item you have already used that you would like to pass along to someone who will enjoy it and use it more than you will. One example is a dress you have removed the tags from and worn twice. You could wrap it up and give it as a "gift" only if you provide another real gift. A regift should be just that: a gift you have never used that you are giving away as though it were a real gift.

Do keep track of who gave it to you first. Writing on The Dollar Stretcher, Joyce Moseley Pierce recommends creating a stash of regifting items you can always use in a pinch. She says, "OK, but keep a small notebook of who gave you what. I had a harrowing experience that involved regifting a pair of earrings to a cousin -- who had given them to me two years before. I forgot. She remembered. And she let me know about it."

Some items are never meant to be regifted. They are a total, dead, instant giveaway that you not only are regifting, but you are too much an ugly duckling to put any effort into it. Here they are:

- Random books

- Mysterious CDs (unless your brother wants the hip-hop version of "Phantom of the Opera")

- Obsolete software

- Cheesy jewelry

- Fruitcake

- Boxed sets of extinct bath products (Jean Nate? No, no, no)

- Videos or DVDs obviously acquired on a street corner

- Socks

- Any appliances or electronic gear the recipient would be puzzled to receive because they probably just got rid of it (including hot-air popcorn poppers)

- Anything with a cassette deck in it.

- Finally, as technology pushes the envelope of regifting possibilities, the chance of looking like an ugly duckling only grows. Do not give a $25 gift card to Barnes & Noble that has $14.56 left on it. Would you give a cake with a slice taken out of it?

Do have the courtesy to clean your regifts. Can you imagine an ugly duckling giving you a rice cooker with a couple of kernels of rice still clinging to it? Some hand-me-downs can be passed off as regifts if the packaging is intact, like the wine glasses you have belatedly decided to share with a loved one. Just wash the lipstick off the rim, okay?

Escalator Etiquette

First things first. When ascending, the gentleman allows the lady to enter the escalator ahead of him. That is because if she falls, he (the peacock) is there to catch her. When descending, the gentleman stands in front of the fair lady. Again, if she falls, he is there to catch her.

Etiquette rules exist to keep the flow of human traffic moving at a steady pace, so people can get where they need to go.

Ugly ducklings that ignore the rules through selfishness or idiocy cause headaches and frustration for peacocks.

Stand On the Right

This applies to escalators city-wide. If you wish to remain stationary, the right side is where you belong. Not in the middle. Not on the left.

This includes your shopping bag(s), too. Forget about taking a cart — or worse, a stroller, complete with infant.

It is obvious, yet despite instruction signs, some folks insist on standing wherever they like. Some people either are in a hurry or cannot stand waiting. The left side of the escalator is their lane.

Think of it as a multi-lane highway: the fast lane is not the place to drive 30 mph or km/h. When you block the left side, you create a traffic jam.

It is bad enough when one person does it, but when a group of ugly ducklings waddle on the same step, they are impeding progress.

Moving sidewalks, however, are another matter. The point of these contraptions is to speed pedestrians through long, flat passageways by augmenting walking speed. Ugly ducklings standing on the left and not walking defeat the purpose.

The elderly and the infirm are welcome to remain still, as long as they stand on the right. Any able-bodied person who stops and stands on the left is an ugly duckling who will not be invited to the peacock party.

Hold the Hand Rail

Simple: should the escalator come to sudden halt—and they do now and again— ugly ducklings not holding the rail are going to pitch forward and do a face-plant on a metal step. If the escalator is full, the ugly duckling has just created a human domino chain.

Remember: you are riding on six tons of moving machinery. Machinery can fail.

Don't Stop At Either End

Some ugly ducklings must be suffering from congenital distraction, because no other explanation makes sense for why they reach the beginning or end of the escalator (or moving sidewalk) and stop dead in their tracks. They must not realize other people are behind them.

At the entrance, stopping is an annoyance. At the exit, it is problematic. Unless the ugly duckling wants folks to shove them out of the way or play leapfrog off their backs, they should open up a space for others to pass. This applies to Mr. Vacillator, as well. Either use the escalator or steer clear of it; but make a decision.

Don't Cut Corners

This pertains to pairs of escalators moving in opposite directions.

Ugly ducklings are notorious for being corner-cutters. These people when wanting to enter or exit make a 90-degree turn and cut across the entrance or exit of the other escalator.

Instead of taking a few steps to head the other way, thereby clearing a path for others wishing to use the escalator, these ugly ducklings disregard good manners.

Elevator Etiquette

Peacocks know that upon entering an elevator, you should stand as close to a wall or corner as possible. This will help them and others distance themselves from one another with a hearty buffer zone. When it comes to body language, you can reduce a spatial invasion if you eliminate large body movements, decrease eye contact and lower your tone and pitch of voice.

The more people who enter the elevator, the more your body language should get smaller. When going to a high floor, it will save everyone from sighing and bumping into each other if you just stand in the back. If you are on one of the lower floors, please stand toward the front.

Elevator Spatial Rules:

1-2 People: Separate

Four People: Each person should take a corner

Five or More People: Face the door, get taller and thinner. Hands, pocketbooks, and brief cases should hang down in front of the body (fig leaf position), do not touch people unless over-crowding forces shoulders and upper arms to touch.

To Look or Not to Look at People

Generally, most people on an elevator are in self-talk mode; thinking about their day or perhaps planning for tomorrow. They tend to gaze at the ground, the button panel, the closed doors, or they may quietly look at something they are holding in their hands. While avoiding visual contact is a means of avoiding interactions, women and men approach the issue of eye contact in this 4 x 4 boxed-in space differently. Men prefer to have no eye-contact with anyone inside the elevator, while the ladies need to know who they will be sharing this small space with, so they will give a quick glance and maybe even flash the giant of all gestures − a smile.

In addition, the most common facial expression seen in an elevator is the "non-expression," which is used by most of us to keep strangers at a distance. The blank stare is probably the only tool we have to maintain our "private space" — it sends the message, "DO NOT DISTURB!"

Rules of Conversation

Any time you are talking with someone on an elevator, take a moment for a reality check. Are you talking quietly or can the people on the outside of the elevator still hear you? Are you an ugly duckling who is dropping profanities or talking about a private issue? Are you noticing the negative non-verbal cues the other people are sending you (bending away from you, wrinkled noses, rolling eyes)?

For the most part, conversations in the elevator are generally not recommended. But if you are the type of person that likes to talk to strangers in line at the grocery store and you must chat with people in the elevator, then keep the topic simple and light, i.e. "I love your coat," "Your earrings are beautiful," or "How about those Yankees (or any other sports team)?"

Finally, when leaving a crowded elevator, remember: last in, first out. There is no need for the men to wait for the women to exit ahead of them. Everyone is anxious to get out, so do not block the way.

Yes, you now have the tools to be a peacock and make your next elevator journey a little quieter and safer for our sanity!

Limousine Etiquette

Peacocks know that limousines are an elegant, comfortable, and dignified mode of transportation. Whether being used for funeral, wedding, or party transportation, practicing limousine etiquette demonstrates class and sophistication. I thank Jeffrey Mudgett, Owner / Operator, Certified Professional Chauffeur, Mudgett Sedan Services, Inc. of Denver, Colorado for this section.

Chauffeured Transportation Industry Overview

In the late 1800's words, describing limousines and chauffeurs, are rooted in private carriages and trains where professional drivers and "stokers" were charged to manage horse teams and steam engines. True to the etiquette of the formal horse drawn coach, a hired driver allowed the owner to relax in luxury. Soon the chauffeur rivaled the senior butler at the family estate.

Limousines and chauffeurs are steeped in history, elegance, wealth, style, influence, social status and image. Automobile manufacturers build "coaches" rich in luxury and design. Some of the high-end vehicles are Rolls Royce, Duesenberg, Mercedes, Cadillac, and Lincoln.

Who is behind the tinted glass? The President of the United States has always enjoyed use of limousines. So, too, have captains of industry, celebrities, and anyone else who wants to convey that special image.

Market Segments:

Corporate

Wedding / Bachelor/ Bachelorette

Prom

Anniversaries

Birthdays

Concerts

Sporting Events

Resort travel

Family reunion

Award banquets

Retirements

Valentines Day

Bringing new baby home

Many more

Expectations of a Professional Chauffeur:

Peacocks know that the proper term for the person driving the limousine is chauffer. Professional chauffeurs take rigorous training in order to ensure that your experience is all you expect it to be.

Chauffeurs always focus on safety. They attend to the vehicle doors, opening and closing them as passengers enter and exit the limousine.

Without passengers seeing it, chauffeurs are prepared with safety equipment (flares, first aid kits, and radio contact with their base). What passengers do see are well-groomed representatives of their companies. Your chauffeur should be well groomed with clean, pressed dark uniform (tuxedo, black suit), company tie or bow tie, name badge, and drivers cap. They should show professional personal grooming, especially, no neck, ear, facial and nose hair with minimal to no cologne, because of being in close quarters.

Chauffeurs are not the "life" of the party. Do not expect them to be the night's entertainment. They will assist with gifts, food, luggage, and decorations. Be sure that they maintain confidentiality: over heard personal information, stays private. If you prefer total privacy, ask the chauffeur to raise the privacy divider, if your limousine is equipped with one. Your chauffeur will be glad accommodate your request when asked and if appropriate.

Your chauffeur should be seen but not heard. He or she should keep conversation to a minimum and speak only when spoken to. Your chauffeur is amenable to positioning the limousine, posing for photographs, providing and serving non-alcoholic beverages. They are proficient in briefly utilizing their customer's camera or video equipment upon request.

Chauffeurs have the ability to mix with other attendees in a comfortable, professional manner, answer business inquires, be knowledgeable about local hotspots, shortcuts, hotels, restaurants, and shops. They should have fast fun facts of local economy, demographics, history and current events.

In terms of top-notch service, chauffeurs may even have popular car cell phone chargers available because their goal is to exceed customer expectations.

Expectations of the Vehicle

When your limousine appears at your home, hotel, airport pickup, etc., it should be impeccably maintained, be mechanically sound, and have good tires. Of course, all aspects of the vehicle must be functional. This includes the radio, lights, privacy divider, and climate control; all features in them must be in working order.

The limousine must be clean inside and out with a fresh smell inside. Note any damage before driving off in the vehicle.

Ensure the seat belts are visible and working, that the vehicle has clean and elegant stemware or glass wear. A properly equipped limousine has an insulated interior ice chest full of bottled water and reading material when appropriate. Some even have a newspaper such as the Wall Street Journal, or elite fashion and fine travel publications.

Expectations of You, the Client

This chapter has focused so far on the limousine and the chauffeur. Now that you are equipped with this information, let us focus on your peacock or ugly duckling behavior.

As mentioned, chauffeurs are generally to be seen but not heard. However, some clients dismiss or minimize their chauffeurs. Chauffeurs appreciate being acknowledged and treated with respect. Hello, please, thank you and "good job" go a long way.

Only ugly ducklings would be involved in any of the following illegal or dangerous conduct:

- Drugs

- Prostitution

- Weapons

- Underage drinking

Those who ride in a limousine respect the investment made by others in a specialty vehicle. A specialty stretched vehicle can cost $250,000 or more.

Peacocks obey the chauffeur and are open to chauffeur's suggestions.

Peacock Behaviors:

- Positive conversation and reflection on the privilege of riding in a limousine.

- Pleasant interaction and conversation

- Opening the doors only when given a verbal "OK" from the chauffeur AND other passengers.

Ugly Duckling Behaviors:

- Opening the vehicle door while in motion.

- Negative conversation and ridiculing others not privileged enough to be riding in a limousine. (Often passengers get judgmental and condescending to those also attending the same event who are NOT in chauffeured transportation)

- Negative conversation about other individuals or groups (rivals, unknowns)

- Standing up through the moon roof while vehicle is in motion

- Throwing anything out of a limousine

- Extending any body extremity outside any opening of the vehicle, ever!

- Excessive movement or rough housing

Tips for Booking a Limousine

- Ask co-workers, friends and family for a referral

- Contact local and national limousine associations and BBB (Better Business Bureau)

- Book early

- Know the event, number of passengers, number of hours, select right size vehicle

- See the EXACT car.

- Visit the company headquarters

- Take a look around

- Does the limousine company have the legally required authorities and insurance(s)

- Verify the alcohol policy

- Does the company have a liquor license?

- Can the vehicle maneuver the pickup point and drop off point? Can a stretch limousine pull in and drive out?

- Ask what is included in service

- Price: Make sure levels of service generally correspond with price

- Tipping: Chauffeurs are typically paid at or close to minimum wage and supplement their income with tips. Chauffeured transportation companies all compensate their chauffeurs differently. In some cases chauffeurs gratuities are quoted as part of the total price 15 –20%. Technically, in that case, chauffeurs cannot expect a tip. Subsequently, employers may or may not pass the entire 15 – 20% tip on to the chauffeur. Some employers hold back tips for auto detailing following the run. Most limousine clients tip their chauffeurs based on the level of service they have received and do not question a 15% service charge (tip) included on their final bill.

- At the same time, other limousine companies will exclude the tip from their pricing schedule as this attracts customers who are shopping around for low prices. Know if the reservationist has included the chauffeurs tip in the quote or not. Enclose the tip in an envelope, if possible. Hand it directly to your driver after completion of your ride.

- Arrival times vary between companies. In the industry "If you are on time, you are 15 minutes late." Weddings typically require an earlier pickup window (30 minutes). Charges start either at the scheduled pickup time or when the client enters the limousine.

You are now equipped with all the tips you need to be the sophisticated peacock when hiring a limousine.

Etiquette for Holy Places

Major religions have specific rules for attendance in their holy places. Peacocks are comfortable because they study and practice showing respect for all religions. Per Wikipedia, here are the rules.

Buddhist Holy Places

Avoid extending your feet towards other people, in particular the bottom or soles of your feet or shoes. Remove your shoes before entering a temple or monastery. "Namaste" (nah-mah-stay) is an appropriate greeting. Women should not offer to shake hands with a Buddhist monk. Women should wear clothing with sleeves or cover their shoulders with a large scarf before meeting with a monk.

Monks wearing the bright orange robes of an ascetic typically practice strict self-denial as a measure of spiritual discipline. They often avoid contact with women altogether.

Christian Holy Places

Men should remove any head coverings in shrines and churches. Women have traditionally covered their heads with a hat or scarf. In Catholic or Orthodox religions, address priests as "Father," nuns as "Sister," and monks (who are not priests) as "Brother." Address monks who are also priests as "Father." Address Protestant ministers as Reverend."

Confucian Holy Places

Business casual attire is preferred at Confucian temples. A bow from the waist is an appropriate greeting.

Hindu Holy Places

Remove shoes before entering a temple or attending a puja (religious ceremony). "Namaste" (nah-mah-stay) is an appropriate greeting, usually done with the hands held together, palms flat against each other. Hindu ministers are called purohita, and may be addressed as "Panditji" (pan-deet-jee). People usually sit on the floor of a temple, or for meetings with purohita or religious leaders. When sitting, do not extend your feet towards the religious leader or towards an altar.

Islamic Holy Places

Remove shoes before entering a mosque or shrine. Women should wear a scarf or other head wrap or covering. Women should not offer their hand when greeting a man. In general, the greeting is "Salaam aleikum," with the right hand placed over the heart.

Jewish Holy Places

Men cover their heads in synagogues. The classic covering is a kepot (skullcap), but any hat will suffice. Women should wear a scarf over their hair. Women should not offer their hand when greeting a rabbi. An appropriate and courteous greeting is "Shalom aleicum, rabbi."

Hospital Visitor Etiquette

Whether a peacock or an ugly duckling, you are always being watched. This includes visiting people in a hospital. You can still be a peacock demonstrating poise and elegance to all, even though they may be distracted because of concern for the infirm. By following these points, your visit with a hospital patient should be happier.

Do	Don't
Leave the gum at home. No one likes to listen to people chew and smack gum.	Wear perfume. Perfume can even gag healthy people.
Only talk about happy situations not about bad news.	Talk about your past illnesses or operations.

Do	Don't
Always check with the nurse before you bring a food present.	Eat food you have brought as a gift to the patient.
Check even if the patient asks you to pop out for a certain food. It might be detriment to the patient's condition.	Sit on the bed; it cramps the patient.
Greet the patient with a handshake. Never hug. Most people when they are sick do not like to be touched, especially if they have had surgery.	Loiter in the room if either the nurse or doctor have to do something. Be polite and leave the room while they are attending the patient.
Be polite and stand if there are not enough chairs. You are only going to be there a short time.	Take the patient for a walk without checking with the nurse first. If you take the patient out of the hospital, let the nurse know.
Only stay a few minutes. The point of your visit is to wish the patient well.	Express negative feelings while you are in the patient's room.
Talk audibly, not too softly or loudly. Increase your volume if you find the patient cannot hear you.	Assume that conversations in the hall cannot be overheard.

Do	Don't
Check to ensure the patient is not allergic to flowers you plan to send.	Assume that your gift suits the patient. If he has just had eye surgery, he will not be able to read a book.
Take a vase along with the flowers, since most hospitals are short on these items.	Expect nurses to arrange your flowers.
Give relatives quality time and privacy with their patient. Sometimes they come from quite a distance.	Overstay your welcome.

Funeral Etiquette

Funeral etiquette is different around the world because of religious and national preferences. This section addresses etiquette for a Western Protestant funeral.

The obituary is in the newspapers. Read it to be sure whether you should send flowers to the church (and if it is satisfactory to send flowers to the family). Some people will have in the obituary: "In lieu of flowers please donate to _____" (it may be the cancer or heart foundation). Out of respect, give what you can afford. You can still send just a sympathy card or flowers to the deceased's family if you so choose.

It is quite common for a wake (sometimes called a visitation) to be held prior to a funeral. The wake offers mourners a chance to say goodbye to their loved one, while gathering together for support. Sometimes the casket will be open and people can actually touch or speak directly to the body.

Most people appreciate the chance to attend a wake. It can provide a sense of closure or acceptance to those who have lost someone.

If you attend a wake, you should approach the family and express your sympathy. As with the condolence visit, it is appropriate to relate your memories of the deceased. If you were only acquainted with the deceased (and not the family), you should introduce yourself.

It is customary to show your respects by viewing the deceased if the body is present and the casket is open. You may wish to say a silent prayer for, or meditate about, the deceased at this time.

The length of your visit at the wake is a matter of discretion. After visiting with the family and viewing the deceased, you can visit with others in attendance. Normally there is a register for visitors to sign.

As for the funeral, you do not have to dress in black, but dress in subdued colors (no bright colors). Black is highly acceptable as many people still prefer it. Most men wear dark colored suits or sports jackets and pants. Never wear jeans or T-shirts. A pair of slacks, shirt and shoes is acceptable.

Mature women generally will wear a hat or scarf when going into the church, but younger women do not have to unless it is Catholic or Anglican.

If the family wishes, they may have a "receiving line" where family members stand so friends can show their condolences. All you have to say is, "I am very sorry for your loss."

There is generally an usher provided by the family or church that will seat you, so stand at the door inside the church or funeral parlor and wait a minute. If no one comes to seat you, seat yourself.

If you must talk, speak in a low whisper, but try to remain quiet. Peacocks know that a funeral is a respectful event.

If you recognize someone, or someone you know smiles at you, do not start up a conversation. Just smile and nod.

There may be an open casket (as well as pictures of the deceased). Watch what others do, as sometimes only family will view the deceased and say their goodbyes (sometimes this is done either the day before or an hour or so before the actual funeral). If others are going up to the casket to say their goodbyes, then follow suit. However, note it is not mandatory that you go to the casket to view the body. If you choose not to go to the casket, step into the aisle to let others pass you. Return to your seat.

The minister will generally start with the Lord's Prayer and perhaps a hymn or two and then allow family and friends to say a few words about the fond memories they had regarding the deceased. The minister may say a few more words and perhaps a few more hymns. (Some funeral parlors display a slide show throughout the funeral.)

The minister will then announce what follows next: where the funeral procession should go (what cemetery), or if there will be a gathering later and its location. Some friends of the deceased may only go to the church or the cemetery or choose to go to both. Some may miss the post-funeral gathering.

Supporting Grieving Families

My friends Wendi Lester and her sister Heidi Brooks dealt first hand with ugly ducklings and peacocks when their beloved brother, Jody Brooks, died suddenly. Wendi and Heidi offer this advice based on their experience.

Wendi and Heidi say:

If the grieving family must travel out of town to deal with the affairs of the lost loved one, consider donating to a charity they have specified or send cut flowers for the event. Sending potted plants or flowers requires the grieving family to have something else to take care of or to transport.

Food is a terrific, thoughtful and valuable gift for the days immediately following the loss, while the family is 100% focused on their loved one's affairs and final services. Non-perishable food, especially breakfast items, is especially welcome. People are often very generous with food and space in the refrigerator and freezer may be limited.

Offer to pick up out-of-town family and friends from the airport, bus, and train station. This will allow the family members who are doing the organizing and coordinating more time to complete necessary tasks, particularly during business hours.

If the deceased family is from out of town, but they plan to do services in town, a list of nearby hotels, funeral homes, donation locations (for furniture and clothing) and government offices may help.

Offering to do a music or photo compilation that could be played before or during the wake is another time consuming task that will require patience (as the family will want to review music and photo selections) and creativity. However, it is extremely helpful to the family and something that they will treasure long after the funeral event is over.

Telling people how to "feel" or how to "be" (for example, "be strong") is not supportive. Everyone grieves differently and everyone needs to feel it is okay to experience the range of emotions that comes with a loss. Offering a listening ear or a hug are kind gestures that let people know you care and that you are there to support them.

When offering your condolences (by email, card, on the phone or in person), share a specific anecdote whenever possible. This is because it is important for the family to preserve the memory of the person who passed. For example, in addition to saying you are sorry, say, "your brother had such a great, friendly spirit. After we met him at your graduation, my mother kept asking about him."

Another example came from my co-worker who had never met him but said, "He sounds like such a great guy who was really invested in the community."

Lastly, if you offer help, and the family accepts it, do what you say you are going to do. They are counting on you. Many people said, "Let me know if there's anything I can do," but those offers did not feel as sincere as specific offers. For example, someone ordered lunch for 10 and had it sent to the house, which was a nice and helpful surprise.

Section 4. Etiquette for Teens

Many of my friends who have teenagers tell me their children care nothing about etiquette until they feel they need it. By the time they realize they need it, it is too late to be polished and cool; because they have either ignored, or have been unaware of, how to proudly strut like peacocks.

The first huge test is when they attend a prom. They spent hours on planning their attire for the big event. Share this section with them so their manners and confidence will be just as polished as their appearance.

Prom Etiquette

Nix the Prom Drama

So what if your high school nemesis shows up in the same dress as you? And who cares if your biggest rival is talking behind your back? Not you. No fits, fights, or freak-outs allowed at the prom. If someone is trying to rile you up, skip the drama queen act. Prom is a night for everyone to just have fun, so just ignore anyone who tries to stop you.

Do Not Wait to Ask Your Date

This goes for guys and girls: If you have even the slightest idea who you want to ask, just go for it. When the prom is looming in the near future, that hottie you have your eye on is going to be snatched up faster than a pair of designer shoes on clearance. Even if the answer is no, at least you will know—and you can come up with a Plan B so you will not be left dateless the night before the prom.

Do Be a Great Date

He may not be your idea of Prince Charming, but he is still your prom date. No matter what your romantic status is, do not leave him hanging by dancing with other people all night or spending all your time gossiping with the girls. Ditto for the guys. Stay with your date.

Don't Primp in Public

No doubt, a night of partying will require some modest touch-ups, such as reapplying lipstick, cleaning up mascara, and fixing your hairdo. But there is a thin line between touching up and giving an overhaul. Take it to the bathroom, but do not spend the whole night there. Prom is about having a great time with your friends.

Do Bring Cash

Just because your date promised to pick up the tab does not mean you should skip the ATM—you never know when you will have to chip in. Then there are the random expenses like gum or late-night snacks. You do not want to have to ask your date to cover every little expense.

Don't Forget Your Manners

If you do not know the dinner drill, here is a basic primer. Guys, let your date choose her seat first and order first. Stand behind her chair and gently push her chair as she sits.

Place your dinner napkin in your lap and keep those elbows off the table. If you are confused about the silverware, here is the rule of thumb: start from the outside and work your way in. The outer fork is usually for the salad, while the inner fork is for the main course. For more etiquette tips, read Wild Woman's Guide to Etiquette: Saving the World One Handshake a Time.

Do Be Polite to Parents

You do not want to spend all night with them (you may not want to spend 15 minutes with them), but you will still want to pay special attention to your date's parents. After all, it is a big night for their little boy or girl. Greet them politely and shake hands with every member of the family. Do not roll your eyes or get impatient if they want to take one picture too many. Remember, lame as it seems, parents totally live for this stuff.

Do Have Fun!

With so much time spent prepping for the prom, you might have forgotten that the prom is actually just one big party. Do not let stress or nerves get in the way of a great time.

But Don't Go Crazy

You want your killer dress to be the talk of the school, not your drunken antics. So even though prom might seem like the right time to do something wild, do not leave your judgment at home. You want prom to be memorable, but in a good way. You want to be remembered as being a peacock, not an ugly duckling.

More Limousine Etiquette

All passengers must agree to behave like peacocks and be orderly and well behaved. Limousine services reserve the right to expel any person from the vehicle and/or terminate the contract in the event of a violation of any of these conditions by any passenger. The use of profanity, lewd behavior, harassment of any type, toward the driver or anyone else at any given time will be cause for termination of your ride. The driver will return you to the pickup address immediately if there is a violation of these rules, and you will not get a refund!

The driver also has the right to, at any time, stop the vehicle and ask a passenger to exit, in the event that the passenger mistreats the vehicle or driver in any manner.

Passengers should act safely and obey all laws, including no drugs or illegal substances. Alcohol consumption by minors (under 21) is absolutely prohibited by law. The customer will pay any fines. The driver has the right to terminate the ride without a refund (if there is a blatant indiscretion on the part of any rider). In addition, it is illegal to stand through the sunroof, so please do not do this.

The privacy window privilege is up to the chauffeur's discretion.

For your safety and comfort, limousine companies will not transport more persons than the maximum legal allowance.

While limousine companies are happy to let you bring personal compact disks (CDs), and other various personal items along for your ride, they do not take any responsibility for items left in the vehicle during or after the completion of your limousine rental period.

A gratuity of 15 to 20% is customary, and it is also customary to enclose the bills in an envelope and hand them directly to your driver after completion of your fare.

Limousine companies understand the sheer delight that limousines offer, but remember to practice proper limo etiquette to ensure a completely care free experience.

Section 5. Epilogue

Now that you have learned how to go forth as a peacock, do remember to avoid abasing and denigrating the inevitable ugly ducklings you will meet in life.

My friend Phil Okrend sums up below what can happen to us when we judge those who we perceive as those ugly ducklings who make us uncomfortable. These are peacock moments of awkwardness. Phil describes how we can turn moments of awkwardness into Moments of Triumph to keep your peacock aura.

Phil says:

What opportunities and positive business connections are lost when we judge, and then exclude, a person based on initial appearances instead of respecting their differences with the intent to build common ground and connection? We can often get in our own way by shutting out an experience before it has the opportunity to unfold. As we enter an era where diversity is the norm in politics and business, we can personally embrace that spirit of diversity by taking the time to understand the differences of another. In practical terms, we can tune into one another through active listening with questions that acknowledge each other's worldview and perspective.

By going deeper, we may find those commonalities that reveal that we are not so different after all. So, embrace those moments you may perceive as awkward or uncomfortable with another, and turn them into moments of triumph. You will also be doing your part to build a better world where all people feel valued and respected.

Phil Okrend, CPCC, JD

Certified Life & Business Coach, www.steppingstonescoaching.com

Conclusion

Remember that practicing proper etiquette speaks volumes about you. It opens doors for job interviews, socializing, building your business and personal network, and building your comfort level for diverse situations.

Let us all get invited to the peacock party.

Index

Other Books by Sharon A. Hill

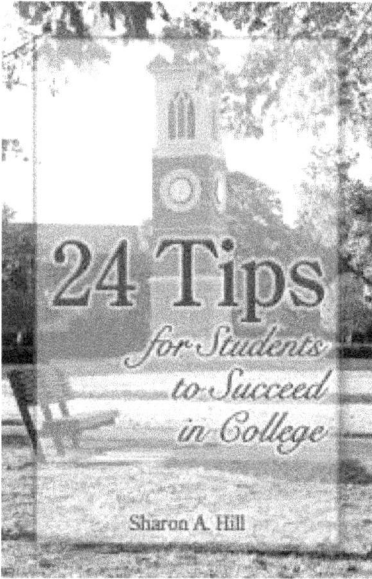

24 Tips for Students to Succeed in College
Sharon A. Hill

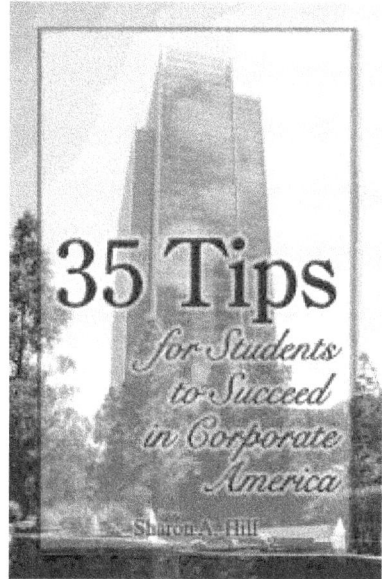

35 Tips for Students to Succeed in Corporate America
Sharon A. Hill

Wild Woman's Guide to Etiquette

Saving the World
One Handshake at a Time

Sharon A. Hill

www.ingramcontent.com/pod-product-compliance
Lightning Source LLC
Chambersburg PA
CBHW021341090426
42742CB00008B/689